AFTERMATH
Preti Taneja

**TRANSIT
BOOKS**

Published by Transit Books
2301 Telegraph Avenue, Oakland, California 94612
www.transitbooks.org

Copyright © Preti Taneja, 2021

ISBN: 978-1-945492-54-9 (paperback) | 978-1-945492-58-7 (ebook)
LIBRARY OF CONGRESS CONTROL NUMBER: 2021942663

COVER DESIGN
Anna Morrison

TYPESETTING
Justin Carder

DISTRIBUTED BY
Consortium Book Sales & Distribution
(800) 283-3572 | cbsd.com

Printed in the United States of America

9 8 7 6 5 4 3 2 1

AFTERMATH

How long
can I lament
with this depressed
heart and soul

how long
can I remain
a sad autumn
ever since my grief
has shed my leaves

the entire space
of my soul
is burning in agony

how long can I
hide the flames
wanting to rise
out of this fire

how long can one suffer
the pain of hatred
of another human
a friend behaving like an enemy

with a broken heart
how much more

can I take the message
from body to soul

I believe in love   *(and I know you do too)*
I swear by love
believe me my love

how long
like a prisoner of grief
can I beg for mercy

you know I'm not
a piece of rock or steel
but hearing my story
even water will become
as tense as a stone

if I can only recount
the story of my life
right out of my body
flames will grow

'Fountain of Fire,' Jalal al-Din Rumi (1207-1273)
TRANSLATED BY Nader Khalili
with Nick Cave refrain

I.

RADICAL

DOUBT

AN EVENT HAPPENS AND

It is a bright morning when the call comes. Everything becomes brighter: like a vision of a nuclear blast in a film. It is as if everything solid has broken into pieces. As if the world has cracked. It is a shivering, an unshakeable sickness. It feels like concrete in the stomach. Shattered and stark as ice on deep water, struck with a blade. Like being held under, lungs filling. Sorrow deep enough to drown in. And this is a failed attempt to say: it feels like being locked in a dark room, screaming. Alone and falling. The repetitive rhythm is not a *glitch,* it is an artefact of pain   repeating. It feels like being constantly watched. It is an assault: it is a wailing. It is being forced into a nightmare without being allowed to sleep. It is everywhere, as if all the masks have dropped. It is living in the real and it is the remembered real. This is a shattering. A 'textbook version' of trauma as an extreme cliché. The silence after an echo of a stone, pounding. It is begging: no one hearing. Like losing a mind while breathing and smiling. Like a hand around the throat. Forced deeper into the wreck of it. A rage. Like raging.

This is the core of the atro-city. The outside world turned inwards.

There is so much violence. It is mainlining butterflies. It is swallowing nails. It is being hollowed. Scraped out. As if saturated with a secret that must only pour from eyes. The wind exists only as pine trees, moving. Trust, the elixir, seeps from our bodies. Always too far away to feel. We cannot stand. There is just skin and hair and fragile bone. It is like being stabbed from the inside. Being held under: struggling, still. Not wanting to move. Holding out a hand, finding nothing. Losing any grip. Being interrogated by buildings, by streets, by your absence, the air. Standing in silence. What is left? It is a heart, broken.

There is no syntax or simile to do justice to this. No metaphor. As if to speak would be more violence.

It was as if I had lost language / been forced / to the outer edge of words

Left with a body that even Antigone
would refuse to hold in her arms

It is the immediate aftermath. *I am living / at the centre / of a wound still fresh.*[1] Inside only silence. I have lost all sense of countable time and all respect for aesthetics, which, Audre Lorde writes, *pertains to things perceptible to the senses,* which *pertains to things material, as opposed to things thinkable,*[2] the unthinkable has happened: it is here. I can only bear this body, these words   heavy, in plea to others' words   as the *I* is not only mine   it belongs to many

Ocean Vuong writes that *metaphor in the mouths of survivors* becomes *a way to innovate around pain*.[3] But language locks in my throat. It is wrong to innovate around *this* pain. My limbs are frozen. Is it futile to dig for the roots of violence? I have nothing to dig with but my fingers, these primitive keys as words the only way in. Metaphor belongs to the Eurocentric sublime: it has no place in this brown skin (which has only ever been understood *in relation to*, as shadow is to light).

An event happens and happens and happens: this is a definition of trauma. Splintering trust in language. This is horror, and horror is piercing. This is terror, and it floods the synapses, freezing all response. Break to gesture. And the gesture of horror is hand over mouth. And the gesture of terror is the blade. And the gesture of trauma is hand over eyes. And the gesture of pain is head in hands. Do not see, do not speak, do not hear. There are acts of such vicious duplicity and damage they turn solid bodies into molten grief.

In moments of deep loss we become as children, trained to seek comfort in the old fairy tales: the fundamental good versus the fundamental evil. We crave the redemptive hope of *the hero's journey*   in the old tradition of linear story   from when we

are born we are immersed   in this the dominant mythic; we
wait for someone to deliver us

But my skin and tongue are dark. My mind made multitudes by
history. Memory as pani   *water* as anagram of *pain*. I experience
love through a porous border. I apprehend faith as the lack of it.
Trust only as its loss. The body is grief, the body is guilt, the body
is doubt, the body is the state   I must write it. I cannot skin
myself. I am shattered: cannot put the pieces down. Cannot speak,
cannot ask you to listen. It would be too much to hope for as the
event has happened, and when *hearing is a form of feeling.*[4]

Is it easier to write fiction, to represent?

An event happens and happens and happens, as wave after wave,
breaking us. My blood turns on itself. I have always known
whiteness / as splitting. I was schooled to know brownness as
shame. The world as experienced keeps turning. I know that
the quiet ones are inside us, waiting, ferocious and bound to
harm.

Something has happened: I no longer believe in the potential
of words to *resist*, to heal or to sing the horizon.

This is the heart of the country of radical doubt: the atro-city
called home.

Its rules were written *in the beginning*. The ivory towers stare straight ahead. Their dizzying heights demand we do not look down. To the unsurvivable depths. Power covers its pale stone   red as the autumn ivy cultivated to hide   the crumbling bricks. Its delighted beauty rises from these foundations: the organising fictions of gender and race. A class system: education, literature as structural harm. Cracking and breaking: law and order, cement of the atro-city walls. Some of its subjects are citizens, and all of us are its subjects.

And its fairy tale goes that violence is born in some bodies, it lies innately within. The ontological categories are: human, *not quite* human, *non* human   That we hide our nature until we choose   We must be forfeit from feeling: from our feeling. We must be punished and banished. Made and remade and nurtured to obey, or reveal ourselves in our *monstrosity*   and when one case *proves the rule*

To create such categorical myths requires, in fact, a novelist's skill. And your suspension of disbelief. The endgame is a child's life and mind. Maybe one day even ours

What does the atro-city fear above all? *The dissolving of distinctions that would separate the inside from the outside; the collapse of the fantasy of sovereignty*[5]

Extreme power is a drug; beckoning solace with the promise of community / tantalising the shine of individual glory /

demanding obedience whilst it peddles death.

The distance from words to violence is infinite, unmeasurable, and intimate and infinitesimal, and felt as relentless until. Inside the gates of the atro-city the threat level is *extreme*

This body is heavy as words   they are *unbearable*. Carry them now through this pale, flat land, the page. To fact / to lie, to grief / to shame. To daring to speak. There is no safety here.

When we speak, no wonder: it can feel like everything shatters.
We can become the point from which things cannot be reassembled.[6]

Turn an imperfect circle: seeking solace in familiar forms now splintered by violence into radical doubt: school, stories, poetry, theory, stories, politics, stories, police and return: to prison, which at most we only apprehend through the hammering *fictions* of the reading room, written, they say, for *empathy* – heavy, heavy my arms reach out, palms open, fingers splayed – but they cannot find yours.

This is a lament for many. Who will gather and hold these fragments?
Who will, O who will?

ORDER, ORDER

'INQUESTS INTO THE DEATHS ARISING FROM THE FISHMONGERS' HALL AND LONDON BRIDGE TERROR ATTACK CASE MANAGEMENT'[7]
with asides, insertions, questions and other patterns repeating

Begin with the facts: A convicted *terrorist* attacked and killed Saskia Jones and Jack Merritt at Fishmongers' Hall on 29 November, 2019. The attacker […] was shot dead by police officers on London Bridge.

No: again.

A *terrorist* incarcerated in a high–security prison appeals his *indeterminate sentence*   He will now be released *automatically*, in a fixed number of years, without parole board assessment

December 2018. He is released. He is living halfway and then alone under myriad restrictions. He had *counter-terrorism* mentors the government contract abruptly ended.   Months pass. No train stations, no trains   no internet access, no trips to London, no   level of *security*   stops what happens next. The oversight of Multi Agency Public Protection Arrangements (Mappa) probation, police, counter-terrorism, *Prevent,* Special Branch, MI5   who read *creative writing*, who read *Cambridge University* programme   (there was none, post release) and with bare discussion, and   the risk downgraded from *very* high   to *high*   *and no one exactly gives permission*   no one *exactly* assesses the risks

he takes the train to London for one day. 29 November, 2019.

Arrives at London Bridge to celebrate five years of Learning Together, a prison education programme.[8] Taking university students into prisons to learn alongside incarcerated people. In minimum, medium and maximum facilities (call it high-security, Category A), learning Plato in Philosophy, the laws of probability, and *creative writing*.

The Justice asked the prison governor: *did you consider the risks of putting people who were potentially violent, manipulative and predatory directly alongside potentially young students in a learning environment*   yes   and the course began

No physical harm came to them there. The deep violence of the prison apparently held outside   the writing room. The

meeting of *writing together*   considered *low risk*   the violence
of the prison where he was known as *emir.* The concentration
on him and his   masks   the violence of the prison, the
breaking   the drug   abuse, the harm   the many serving
long and life there   the violence of the prison only seen in
reflection   the *emphasis* on counter–narrative   on hope

He took part. He was enthusiastic, did more learning, became
a mentor on the probability   course   he was released. He
was welcomed / encouraged / writing / allowed to keep close
to the education programme, it was considered *a protective factor*
(there were no others)   the only thing he had   apart from
the gym.

He sits through the morning. After the break, he straps knives
to his hands, wears a fake bomb vest   he made   and murders
two people at the event. He injures more. He is apprehended
by *citizens*   He is shot twenty times by police on London
Bridge.

No: again.

A British youth,   *who all the teachers liked*, is *bullied at school*
though *tried to fit in*. He is involved in racist incidents, and in
violence   turns *recluse*[9] and is done with the place by age
14. At 15, as his sister's house is raided by police, they find
jihadi leaflets, and so on   he faces local news cameras to

say he *aint no terrorist*, that everyone around knows him. He
goes to Pakistan for time and returns to gangs   he   never
goes back to school *and no one can corroborate*   those lost
years   whether he was excluded / expelled / just didn't show
up   no one can state   the details   now ask   *how is it that*

He is *radicalised*   into violent ideology   by known hate
preachers who emphasise *education*, (you know the *immigrant
drug*).   He becomes part of a group   wants to prove   calls
what he does *just fundraising*, or simply spreading the word.
They plan to bomb the London Stock Exchange / under the
guise of *education*   found a *jihadi training camp* in Pakistan
some say Kashmir   the difference interchangeable in the
press/ is *redacted*. He is 19

And sent to high-security prison. Spends eight years   some
of it (accounts vary how much) deep inside *the prison within a
prison* / some of it (though less than he claimed) in solitary /
in proximity to violence / the killer of Fusilier Lee Rigby /
Anwar al-Awlaki   wanting to *impress*   he begins to radicalise
others / is dispersed / is dispersed / is a bully / is violent /
hates *criticism* / denies harm or any *culpability* / wants *learning* /
never finished school / takes a distance learning course/ *creative
writing* / is dispersed to HMP Whitemoor / maximum / high
/ security.[10]   Built under the blades of a wind farm in a
flat, waterlogged place called East Anglia. A one-hour drive
from Cambridge University where some bright students gain

admission to life in the once-drowned world   where waves
of land mirror the long-receded sea   and those who taught
him face to face   were not informed   he was categorised
A: the highest risk possible in a Category A prison: among
the most high-risk men in the country   inside the heart of
violence there is a cell

Here is a question from the jagged edge: how far must we go
back to find a beginning? We cannot ask why (the answer will
break us), but only, hearts broken, ask *how.* He was released.
No one agency gave him permission· to go to London. No
one denied it either. He said he enjoyed *creative writing*   this
was given as evidence   of hope. The only speech possible
is lament

Who will gather and hold these fragments? Who will, O who will?

Deradicalisation system untested / *desistance* as difficult as staying
off spice / or crack no parole board assessment / the *forensic
psychologist* warned and warned that *compliance* was a danger sign
/ that isolation was a danger sign / that lack of employment
/ or a gang was a danger sign / he was   *presenting* positive
behaviour the *probation officer* said, towards the end of his
sentence / in the prison classroom / he was released

Straight into a town / no de-categorisation from A to B to C
to open prison D / no slow acclimatisation / no re-socialisation /

just some education courses while inside starting with *creative writing* it / coincided with a change/ He had a sense of self-importance / he told the gym he went to about his offence / he could not use the library computers when his mentors disappeared / could not search for a job / could not get one / would be on licence for 30 years.

I can write that the body can never be laid down. I can write the fact of its *knives as hands*, as I now suffer them in dreams. Its crimes are its legacy, its only title. Call it liar / reader / murderer/ monster / call it *terrorism*. (Now imagine – the first freedom of fiction – that *terrorist* as a body. What body do you see?) The question of what lies under the skin: silent, electric, potential; call it life   and the memory of listening, trying to learn

The forensic psychologist reported that *he showed no sense he had committed any crime.* No criticism ever allowed without resentment. He *got a kick from learning*, she said, *from being highly regarded.* That prison *had exacerbated his risk.*   And the prison is a violent place/ that can be believed

      He goes on to   *who read her report and took it in?*

We wake to the thought every day: good people have been killed. We wake again and the dead cannot speak. Except through metaphor, memories, signifiers, sounds. All stories can be read as possible beginnings, as the event repeating

MI5 opens an investigation. This was not known to his probation. His category was downgraded from *very high risk*. They know   he was known as an *emir*   on the wing   for inciting disruption   writing violent poetry   throwing himself on the nets   between prison floors   in 2013.

He was a British Pakistani youth *radicalised* young. In 2009 he is photographed with a well-known extremist[11] whose emphasis is on power and on *education*. Preying on the damage caused by Western political and military intervention. Playing on personal pride, the injuries of everyday   racism. This was not known by his brother.

He preaches in public   he boasts on a market stall   and under surveillance is caught   speaking   about funding and establishing *a jihadi training camp* in Pakistan-administered / Azad Kashmir – he is the son of a retired taxi driver – *who told him his life after prison   was not harder   than his was when he first came to the UK* – he the second youngest of seven – out of home / with a friend / in a gang / his sister – after *leaving* school at 14. He was married to a woman he never lived with or *knew*. He wants to be *known*. He says he wants *to write* – he has planned – is held in segregation   sometimes in isolation   in prison he says he is an avid reader of novels   in prison   rife with abuses, narratives, violent gangs, bullying, all the intensity of outside distilled to cells   kudos for recognition, praise, to be a leader, radicalising others   where more and more might succumb

He is violent as radical form – it is a way of gang life in the prison.[12] He says he is mocked for watching pop music videos – he meets more violence inside – he attends the government's deradicalisation programme[13] – *to make the choice every day, as an addict must want to abstain, must not choose harm or to harm – the harm is always latent – and can only be prevented* – he says he is celled next to 'Britain's most dangerous' offender – a man named Charles Bronson   whose own life has been made into a film[14] who tells him *just do it* or something like that – by which he means attack. He is still *forcing others to convert* as he excels in the education programme he is in   he is made a mentor   a prolific *writer*

These details are not for juxtaposition or titillation   or to pathologise prison or people   but real. His prison is a divided place. His mind – doubled locked – a hall of dark mirrors reflecting the bias of whoever he was speaking to back to them now again under decades of splitting the pressure to be *someone* he chooses

Probation visits him for eight minutes and registers nothing of concern. He takes cash out, goes to the market and buys knives. He takes apart his Xbox and makes a fake bomb vest out of a slimming belt. And kills two people at a celebration of education, the creative writing seminar / the poetry workshop he kills two people and hurts more   he knew   he always pushed to be downgraded to a lower risk

We cannot ask why no one knew what they say they didn't know. He was calm / pleasant / blank faced / always polite his handlers said though   he had been written up as *deceptively compliant*   We cannot think anymore: *When someone shows you who they are, believe them the first time*[15]   We cannot ask why this happened, but only, hearts raging, ask *how*   He came to be

He was 19 when he was convicted *a terrorist*. He went to prison for eight years. Entered the *subculture* (the legal term for uncivilised, for not like *us*)   the spice. Glorifying high risk, *terrorists* and their crimes.   He nurtured these histories political   excluding   what he would not admit   became, it seemed, towards his release   a model man. Some saw good change, extremism always present underneath.   He came out into a world that responded to his *stories*, to probation   and Prevent officers lacking enough experience   a world that had been, in the interim, carefully cultivated to become a full decade more hostile than the one he left.

He has forfeited the right to a full backstory, the fiction writer's gas and air.

In 2013 he was found   in prison stockpiling chemicals for a bomb. They found a loose razor blade taped to the underside of his locker   in 2017   and the address of a prison governor he took part in the government's Healthy Identity Intervention (HII) deradicalisation scheme   while influencing inmates to kill and harm others   and Intelligence records, (though this was never seen)   that he *was playing the system*,   his tactic was *false compliance*   in reports   inside   on the wing. Some of this was known   but never passed to his teachers who had young students in a high-security room for hours with others and with him.

Living alone, tagged by the state. Wearing new clothes. On-brand boots. Under many counter-terror restrictions he barely knows about. Alone.   In a post-industrial town. He never hides his index offence   is perfectly compliant   raises warnings when he might breach licence conditions   unwittingly for example   he was given an internet-capable mobile phone he reported it   his mentors all underestimated him   little state help   ego demanding   ideology constant, playing Xbox all day and walking around town

The counter-terrorist probation guy   was *concerned   that there was a celebration   that a terrorist offender had*   changed his life   he didn't want him to take on the identity of an ex-terrorist (*speaking / writing* and so on)   He was reassured when he was made aware of the *creative writing aspect*.   As if that was a symbol of something   and thought   *not many with his background are fortunate to get into universities such as Cambridge*   that this would be potentially positive for his sense of belonging to society.

Scant community support: the gym owner, the job centre, were kind. He was not allowed to go on a dump truck licence course. *Creative writing* was considered a sign of *hope*   Those who should not have *come into contact* with him will never be the same again. After years of routine, inside, split   between praise and denigration, and the violence of it, no longer in the classes where one could   prove something to oneself,   feel the respect of peers, and this is true.   Experts   around him hearing only his stories   his theological mentor called him a *compelling storyteller*   but did not know (because he was not officially told)   his offending history   preying on hope goes *two ways*   the horror is in the depth of intention, the intimate violence   the failures to read the signs   O my heart

In the heart of the citadel his image was featured as a story of achievement, the face of the prisoner education programme. He was far from it   *writing a play* about a knife attack MI5   considered it simply *rehabilitative* (the rest will be redacted) *as no one admits   that in retrospect anything could have been different*

Language doubles and folds as a witness remembers him saying, minutes before he went to prepare, something like, *he had been involved with a group of people who had been leading him down the wrong path, and he was essentially turning another way, or a different way   it was words to that effect*[16]

I am looking for some responsibility. I need some accountability. I won't be complicit in denial. Don't be complicit in denial. Please don't be complicit in denial. I am looking for some integrity   Or don't say their names again

He was a radicaliser, a violent extremist. Passed around the maximum security prison estate to disperse his influence, he landed at HMP Whitemoor, a place with a complicated history. Holding terror. Of abuse of solitary. More *Muslims* there since 9/11. Only a handful of *terrorists*   mixing with others   making them   in the search for peace inside, safety, community, brotherhood, meaning a life sentence – time *is* the punishment. There is also the epidemic   violation of dignity. There was an extreme problem, it was reported, before he was sent there. There was a history of violence and unsettling need. Hope   that education can change

He was released straight into a world he was born into helped to make   more bitter, more scared, more split, more racist since his incarceration. There was survival, and there was routine. There was no more education. There was nothing left.

Many who vouched for his release told the court later: he was *driven by violent ideology*   and a constant requirement for *endorsement and praise*   he always intended to do something, he was clever enough to *game the system*.[17] Meaning everything

he seemed was nothing but *fiction*   while everything he did
gave the lie to his words

Former *Guardian* columnist Erwin James, ex-prisoner, convicted
for murder, whose recounting of his own life story sometimes
leaked into *fiction*, writes, *Few people in prison are strong enough to*
be themselves. *Everybody on a prison landing is a play actor,*[18] is it
a question of survival – the attempt to control – under forces
you cannot control. Others call *taqiyya*, the religious permission
to dissemble (he denied it, and denied it and denied it)   and
prison is a place of stories within stories: as currency   as at
school   what you say about yourself and what you show is
a way of   *passing*   time to live with yourself   find status
there was evidence from a *prisoner*   he would 'return to his old
ways' upon his release   that he was 'planning an attack'   the
source considered 'low grade'   MI5 knew he was going to
London   they said they wanted   to test his mindset   *the*
rest is redacted   the inquest evidence said.

He did not want to go / he changed his mind. He asked for
a police escort, for his own *pastoral care*, so as not to break his
licence conditions   he was wearing a tag   it would have
been triggered underground.   The programme also made the
request   *I cannot justify two police* the answer came, *have a good*
day   He said he wanted to mentor others for *deradicalisation*
he prepared to attack while on the train

It was a bright winter day. A celebration planned of the hardest work done in the most difficult conditions the atro-city can manifest   within its own borders. The purpose of prison is the underlying question

If you say punishment your sense of degradation must answer to this: how far are you prepared to go? How far   down inside   the places most people never see, hear from, want to think of, would you go?

He was tackled, he was wearing a coat. He said he had a bomb. He said he was waiting for police   *He did not look particularly bothered or psyched up.* He did not look *particularly angry.* He did not seem to have *any particular expression* on his face   the witness said

We cannot imagine that day. It should not be imagined. It began as a marker of hope and trust: the longed for, most difficult of bonds, forged from fierce work in the meanest of worlds.

It is nine years since a report damns the treatment of Muslims in UK prisons, where 1 per cent of a rising 10,300 people are inside for terror-related offences, where risk of *radicalisation* or entrenching of views is high, where desist and disengage programmes are in process but have weak foundations and have never been tested: the accepted markers for *radicalisation* easily deflected   by their opposite effect   and he was inside for that, with 14 warning signs of recidivism   he had hit them all   still no one sounded the alarm   by the time he got on the train

It was Friday, 29 November, 2019, twelve days before yet another bitter general election was scheduled,[19] and in the dog days of a vicious, xenophobic Brexit campaign, a racist resurgence fed by those in power in government, their voices on the radio, the TV, the internet, their white cold *patriotism* their fantasy of an indivisible *sovereignty* returned ten-fold in violence *as rhetoric* that   split the country almost clean in half.

He was released straight from high-security, *one of the 70 most dangerous men in the country*. And this could have been known by the education programme, but the information was not asked for   instead there was   *a lack of adequate oversight*. A *break of communication*. People were *inexperienced* and they were *overworked*. And these are the statements given to the court. By August 2019, he had stopped writing. He was not prevented from going to London. He sat with others at circular tables in a fine old building at the heart of the city that morning. He did not take off his heavy coat

There were senior members of *counter-terrorism* and of the *criminal justice* system there. There were men and women, artists, teachers   there was a driving   ideology behind the Cambridge University programme   its prestige   its mission. There were academics and young volunteers; there were event staff. There was a *creative writing* and story-telling workshop. As a writer he had already experienced this rush: *stories can make us feel free.*

The activity (*education*) and where it took place within the prison was considered *low risk*. The prison governor was studying criminology at Cambridge University   there was   hope   as counternarrative to such harm   there were stories being taken as research and relayed   We cannot ask why this happened. Only, hearts broken, ask *how*   he made a video with the education programme earlier that year, praising it, for impact.   A long *research interview* was also   conducted, the probation officer did not receive the notes   and would anything have changed?

There was no security check to enter Fishmongers' Hall. A thing he could not have anticipated   the London Metropolitan Police did not know/ were not *informed*   he was there

Past noon. People on the terrace, upstairs, talking, making their way back inside. The conference, beginning again. He went to the ground floor toilets and readied himself with what he brought with him: a fake bomb vest he had made from Xbox cables, from empty plastic bottles. Two large kitchen knives, which he taped to his wrists.

Before police shot him 20 times on London Bridge, he was tackled by a group of men who were in the building but didn't know each other.[20] Their stories are in the muscles on their arms, the lines on their faces; their instincts tuned by long experience, their desire to protect those they knew. Some ex-incarcerated. One on day release. It is possible to be inside for murder and outside to save lives. The *hero's journey* comes at bitter cost

By then, he had attacked. Screaming alerted those upstairs. They had worked with him for years. He critically injured some of them. Two of them, he killed.

Saskia Jones, 23, *who battled to improve the lives of others […] and was driven to make real changes in the world. She researched sexual violence and worked in a Rape Crisis Centre. She hoped to become a detective working in victim support.*[21]

Jack Merritt, 25, who believed in the possibilities of shared community, and education, and rehabilitation. Who worked for social and racial justice. Kind, funny, compassionate, driven, a mentor to many, an excellent trainer of trainers. No writing could express the life of him. Everything you can read about him is true. Jack was the programme co-ordinator for Learning Together, for its *creative writing* course

The man who killed them   was prolific, showed off his reading knowledge   he craved recognition   He planned and prepared, and came to London   every system failed When he came out of the bathroom, *knives as hands*, Jack was already bleeding out behind him. The witness in the cloakroom saw   her shock   made her think it was a theatrical *re-enactment* or something like that   the other gestured to her to keep quiet.[22] He went towards Saskia.

He stabbed five people. He killed Saskia. He killed Jack. He made a bomb vest   it was *a convincing fake*

'He' was Usman Khan.

For twenty hours across a semester in Whitemoor prison in 2017, I taught him creative writing. The craft of fiction. And taught the course again for two years after that

I think he would have killed any person associated with prison that he could reach that day.

He told the men trying to stop him he was *waiting for police*. He wanted to die like that. [23]

Now go to bed awake. Now dream, eyes open as if on high alert.

DISENFRANCHISED GRIEF

When I think of that time, I think of a fingerprint, lines tracing around each other outwards from the small, intimate core. At heart the family, lovers, the friends and colleagues, spiral outwards, back inwards as you try to   catch yourself in freefall

There is a hierarchy to grief. It is profound and right to observe it, especially when deaths happen publicly and violently, when such people as Jack and Saskia, who were just beginning their work and lived with the brightest hope, are killed. Especially then. The beloved young belong to the ones who hold them closest. First and foremost to the intimacy of deep feeling, scent of childhood, growing up, sun holiday. Sound of their footfall, their phrases, the taste of their jokes, trick senses of smell and sight.

Those who are left now must   transmute their loss into objects suddenly so precious: necklaces, sunglasses, which yield to the way they laughed: light on water, a certain song. These dear fragments synechdoches of the left-behind. Then they become words, spoken, relayed, written down.   A collage of a life. When they open their mourning to the world, it is by kind invitation.

But if grief is a spiral so is guilt. Now for some they bond   as double helix in the cells

Survivor's guilt is felt by those who were invited but did not go to the event, or were not in the same room as where the attack took place; or did not fight the attacker; or were standing near but could not help those hurt; or even those close enough to look into the attackers eyes, and speak to him, and say *stop.* Because *we* did not die, we can suffer that sense that we have less legitimacy to grieve   it seems without end

Some write and apologise for not responding to the invitation to Fishmongers' Hall, as if they now feel they should have been there, if only to have put their own lives at risk alongside those whose were. Perhaps wanting to have been closer to the feeling that it could have – or should have – been them. Through all of the long months that come, for many that feeling sustains. There should be many words for these kinds of sorrow, these kindred feelings, for us as kin.

And in the bright, cold morning in the atro-city, circling the towers of the University, the whorls of cobbled stone, this grief spirals outwards, and catches all who knew Jack and Saskia well, through work, or slightly, or as image. I did not have the chance to know Saskia, I think of her ambitions   in *victim support*   her life touches so many, whether they know it or not. As they do their shopping, visiting, touristing around. And Jack seems everywhere, and Jack is gone. Jack grew up around here. He worked in the local pub; the florist says her daughter was a bargirl at the same time. He had a summer job at the punt operator's: the plumber says his son worked on the punts with him. Flowers in plastic begin to appear in those places. Silent offerings. Both Jack and Saskia studied and found parts of their vocation here. There is a sense that everyone has died, yet here we are, still moving. My eyes constantly sting in the cold.

Those of us carrying the other   cannot find comfort or rest. We cannot speak of the disappeared, the dead, who is horror, who has inflicted terror and horror. There is only this: the parabolic descent. *Dive into the wreck* of what was still a life, and what ruins of life it left. The possibility of a whole life after that

This is grief as exile. From the pure sorrow that one can have when someone one loves dies. It has the sternest edge. It is illegitimate, transgressive. Laced with something more

There is a desire to be quiet, forever: to be so angry as to rage, and at the same time, to hold everyone close, even closer.

Living surrounded by inanimate objects becomes unbearable and absurd. I stay out of my kitchen, away from the knives. (And did the chapel bells continue to mark time: the quarter hour, the half, the hour, the work day, the 'day of rest', as they must in prison?) Even the slightest moment of natural sound – a cat purring, a bird singing (in December – do I remember that right?) seems more necessary, yet more remote.

Face this feeling as a monster turning to eat itself. Repeating the turns. It has its own language I have not yet learned: it has its own grammar. It is a feeling without a word, without a name. It is not grief, or shock, betrayal, or guilt: not only. It is *culpability*   where it lies

He was a guarded man. I taught him fiction   now left with so many stories   what was apprehendable   what was trust in those who invited me in   and what was known about him that I was not told of, while   students   were in prison and in my care   though this did not happen in prison, it was partly made there   and how any of it was able to happen the way it did at all.

    Now, I am locked inside   *what if*   language fails me

A group gathers in a fine college room not unlike the one at Fishmongers' Hall. We sit in a circle. We have a few hours in this space, but time goes around. In this collective of humans doubled down with difficult knowledge and sickening doubt (this nameless feeling), everyone looks long-eyed, as if we can see each other, and beyond each other. As if we are looking through each other: to the dead that are to come

People begin to speak. I hear how symptoms echo from body to body. Sleeplessness. Recurring scenes. Tears. A sense of breathlessness, and *what now.* There is kindness in small moments as we listen to each other, as we make a circle to breathe.

Months later, I will learn the phrase *disenfranchised grief* – a particularly difficult form of loss to overcome. *The majority of cases involve personal decisions made. Such loss often creates a sense of shame or guilt […] making it difficult to openly mourn, discuss or cope with the actions that have created the loss.* I think of the decisions I made, to teach. The vulnerability   of the creative writing room, the requests I made   so I could keep the students safe   never answered by authorities.   The sense I had of each student. Who was posturing, who needed approval, who was writing trauma? All of them. The perfect ones, I recognise presenting to know everything, needing to prove perfection, to hide the opposite damage *I recognise you I*   sound the internal alarm. Anger that there was no one to tell about this, wondering, in any case, who would have listened.   Not trying hard enough.   No shared backstory allowed   while walking through prison corridors: I hold this rage as grief, as a breaking point. As   disenfranchised from   speech by those who will not hear. And move from that to think of the men and the many inside: disenfranchised of their right to vote by the rule of law. Language mirrors, as patterns repeating, transmutes from them to us. Now we are held   a community of the lost.

That I am writing a lecture, an essay, a memoir, a story   is a fiction I tell myself. Time strung out; time withholds   it will not conform to endemic structure. Unruly connections fuse and break   these moments defy narrative cohesion, which offer no protection in a state of going mad

VIOLENCE AS TRAUMA AS FORM

You know that fragments are often used in writing to evoke split consciousness; the near familiar; uncanny; a mind trapped in confusion; intoxication; in chains of memory; in pain. You feel this and read them as a prose poem, a novel, an essay, as something that someone, a writer, a professor, a lecturer (maybe even me), has taught, that you can and should understand them as an expression of seeking. For the whole. To reconstruct feeling for life through this form. Yes, from Roland Barthes to Maggie Nelson, from JG Ballard's *Atrocity Exhibition* to the lyric precision of Claudia Rankine: you encounter this form.

The second person in fiction is an empathy device: it can bring the sense of the other closer than the first, and it can distance, too. As if the reader is alive inside the text or is the text, as traumatic event, recounting – to re-order as a way of sharing – all these tiny shards.

And yet do you listen between the gaps for the obedient /
deviant, the brown female voice? She is the ghost in the narrative
machine whose whispers are in a language I barely conceive.
It is one we are not taught to hear, and so we cannot feel for.
Brown women speak in service, or to honour or bring shame.
It is natural you should find her (version of) the story almost
impossible to take, and even less possible to trust.

She is an unreliable narrator — fiction says — cartographer of
narrative as betrayal. But who decides she is unreliable? Is it
you? Is it culture? Is it criticism? Is it form? Does this form
not fit her body, the mind as forced to split / say between two
points on a compass, two territories on a map?

You are used to reading trauma as an *essay*: an attempt to say — no,
it is a fact. The expectation is to begin with sensation: to centre
the narrative *I*. It is literary, it is tradition: it is considered the form.

But the surface of the page is irrefutably white. Writing makes
me hyper-visible: so much remains unspeakable. This is trauma
as definition.

I need a different map, I need other words. To face the violence
and what made it   I need other armour, to read another
way. Adrienne Rich wrote decades ago about the wreck of
a different kind of harm,   of women seeking resolution,
risking life to meet the future   I, dark woman, alive to

danger   read her now in that way of desperate seekers as *a book of myths*, as if she left them for me to find, as if she knew that this *other* moment might come. *Cameras* captured it, *the knife blade*; I take a breath and prepare. With my own *body armour*, only words   skin like rubber to dive, clumsily, *absurd* as if wearing *hired flippers*, to face   *the grave and awkward mask*.[24] He is waiting. Inside my nightmare as I am now awake

Rich speaks, and I recognise (as I might be mad, or as the faithful believe they can interpret commands from the divine) that

This is the place.
And I am here, the mermaid whose dark hair
streams black, the merman in his armored body.
We circle silently
about the wreck
we dive into the hold.
I am she: I am he[25]

Between s*he and he* a thousand million   lands and miles, rituals, laws and chances, settling them into levels and streams divergent tributaries which meet

here it seems   when she reads the reports that says that in England, young criminal Pakistani men *from certain areas* have chaotic family lives because of the towns and the *chances*, young Indian women from certain backgrounds have better *chances* and that word *chances* holds a history of something, but no one will teach you what   Locks them together it is   the nature

of *divide and rule*   Time has brought them to this moment
say two hundred years and 1947   and everything that came
after: the colonisation of land, the splitting   into her mother's
India and his mother's *Pakistan*;

    and Kashmir between   the denial of trauma
    of British shame   in our making becomes
    a forcing in   how to play your passing
    until you might survive   or break
    I could call it my past,
              but it is hers / it is his.

They circle inside me, threatening: sometimes quiet, sometimes
keening   I cannot hold them here.

She: British Asian − *Indian*[26] (the best category of immigrant)
was one of the perfectly good children, you think you know
them: from the quiet nerds with determined parents that they
write for TV.   *Passing was subconscious*, not only telling white
lies as natural as singing bedtime songs never in English, never
simple nursery rhymes   prayers in the gurudwara, the small
temple at home but only on festival days understanding that we
cannot speak about what we do not know we should mourn:
colonisation; while we learn at home that *time as a straight line
is a monstrosity.*[27] In her unspoken mother tongue there is a
revolution   as yesterday repeating as tomorrow: the single
word is *kal* − I will italicise − as the speaking animals of stories
might

When she is young she becomes aware her parents' stories are never legitimised in the atro-city; she apprehends this as she is meant to: as a kind of shame. She does not speak the critical language,   and thinks she can hide her skin under a cloak that takes the form of straight grade As. Thinks that these might also be stitches: keeping the body in place between two worlds, keeping the body in place. They protect her at home and win her safety / as they enrage the teachers who cast her over   and over   as 'The Poor Girl' in their nativity play. They cover all such *micro* aggressions; they soothe all wounds   while making invisible   the *minor* rebellions against *remember whose beti you are.* They allow her the taste of a 'Western' life (wearing *jeans*, hooking up with pale, long-haired boys after school, who wept only when *Brothers in Arms* played on the radio; as the cherry on the joint burned where it landed and the homemade bong doubled up as a vase), those tiny piercings   reported on by the beloved corner-shop aunties, bravely overlooked by hard-working, tax-paying, education-*obsessed* (as the keys to the kingdom), first-generation parents   who were so proud when she fulfilled the dream

This is a standard story of repeated arrival, as origin event. You have read it before and will again. The struggle into being, becoming someone *good*   assimilation as aspiration   in the sense of *breathing*

It can end in high visibility called *success*, the keys to the citadel, the seat of power; the star turn   *I grew up in the vast encircling presumption of whiteness – that primary quality of being which knows itself, its passions, only against an otherness that has to be dehumanized*[28]

that must only write its *debut* fiction as a beautiful, immigrant *bildungsroman* towards the sovereign light. (And here Empire's ideology meets fiction editors, meets marketing executives, published again and again as *novel*: and this is a definition of trauma.)

I grew up in white silence that was utterly obsessional. Race was the theme, whatever the topic.[29]

Perhaps now is the time for an offering: the anecdote of feeling. The confessional makes the bond between writer and reader. It helps you feel what *I* write has truth. And risk that you might now have begun to trust the text itself. I'm showing you my position, the place where the writing comes from. There's a reachable safety in it, and in bringing you. It offers the comfort that the specificity of singular experiences have only to do with me, to whom they happened and happened. Linked to the moment of you: reading these words. Enabling you to be free with just pity

That singularity is a fiction: I have to tell you it is narrative as lie.

I entered the citadel, studied Theology *and comparative religious studies* (Hinduism, Islam) as an undergraduate, full of hope *and gratitude* to pass through heritage gates.

In this storied place, every green blade of grass is carefully tended. Every meal is three courses and served on china. The river wends to Rupert Brookes' a hero's journey. For gazing at clouds and for deep reflection. Daffodils bloom in April. In the summer, swans glide the river, cows graze out on the Backs. Autumn brings its russet and gold. There is feasting in winter. Criticism is considered high culture; making art is a pass-time, not formally taught as a practice. Here, there is no rage, only production of the best. The logic of racial capitalism is coolly serviced; it is entrenched. It almost repeats by itself, she felt it as an undergraduate but did not know it then

I know now that stranger: I was cast outsider. Learned the language, rules of passing and was permitted and pushed to scale the towers to a certain height, or balance on their strong parapet. Gratitude for that makes me tremble almost to losing my footing

Any exception proves the rule. The rule is set in stone, though people come and go.

I returned thirteen years later. While I worked on my first novel, I taught poetry and close-reading for a short time, made aware over dinner at 'high table', how I am encountered

I know that in the towers of the atro-city, fascists write poetry and form is praised. That creative writing does not mean goodness: the text is a formal violence. That one can research race and racism, or quote poets, revolutionaries of colour out of context   *as if to prove   your solidarity as   diversity of thought*   and keep my head down, so as to never look up around the table

One can sit on admissions committees: admit nothing. An hour across the flat lands there is a high-security prison, where more Black and brown men are committed each season than will ever access the humanities here.

Warning: this narrative may succumb to kinship of skin and tongue: as writer and reader are prisoner of the text, as teacher and student can be in the classroom. As the position of the child of colour   is to learn how to hide, and then how   to *pass*, to misdirect with fictions of self   before we learn *the language the form*; before we find our fates; as *the good immigrant   rarely in culture* but more likely:

    in the civil service
    as NHS doctor, or lawyer or accountant,
    a postmaster, corner shop owner as proud as cliché;
    as youth worker   social carer   community sewa
    as mill worker, balti maker, coffee shop barrista,
    or porter, or chicken shop x Uber driver
    or   *as the terrorist*   is underwritten by history, and
overwritten by two dominant narratives that   in myriad shifting forms   have absolutes that threaten either side.

In the atro-city the diktat is passed down to all good citizens: there are whole bodies of peoples whose stories are not known, that are considered *unspeakable, unmournable, unreadable*.

This is not a confession. This is not a testimony. This is the moment before the frame is exposed. *This is a lament, not for one, but for many not yet born*.

Still. There will always be a prison workshop, where she taught story-making. Inside that room.

He: British Asian – *Pakistani / Other.*   He shared his literary knowledge in class. He worked at his writing. He said he read canonical novels. He said he had plans for work, for writing, for life after release.

People saw his creative writing as a sign of *rehabilitation*, even of possible *deradicalisation*. It was simply, like many, that he valued the form, a conduit for control and self-expression: the art of convincing others   a version of his extreme drug. Now she doubts   Does making art, wanting to be an art-maker make *anyone* less likely to harm?

It is possible to teach craft and yet to know   that making art signifies nothing. Except the human imperative to express a life force and to say

   – *this is what I imagine. I know: I was there.*

Now we are here, *Jack is dead and Saskia,* and what comes now

Maybe he always meant everything he said and did and thought. All of it, and all of the time, and at the same time, until he made his final choice. Time is the worst punishment we can give (where death is not for us to inflict). Now we are left with it   While I taught him the effect of writing fiction for example without full stops

There is only silence, only loss. In the recognition of a history of splitting   there is a radical shame: say doubt. The verdict is he always knew and always lied. Which means his greatest skill was *passing*: he was a product of the state. That we can be both alive and dead at the same time. And while we are breathing do we even know which is which?

This moment feeds on myths: that all *values belong to one faith, the other is always to be harmed.*   It feeds the fiction *that a home, a family, a school, a police, a prison, an intelligence agency, a university, a Home Office, makes us safe*   his actions both prove and disprove   any rhetoric of punishment   any argument for expansion; can I still be determined to hope? The state is aroused to feed on grief and fear   so many more will be lost

I am heavy with this body. I am locked inside it. I open the book at random. The poet teaches me the lesson – the condition of *freedom* – as

The loneliness of the liar
Living in the formal network of the lie.

twisting the dials to drown the terror
beneath the unsaid word[30]

Everything he said about his journey into violence was plausible / some of it happened: the injuries of everyday racism, school dropout / exclusion, surveillance, police harm, big politics he played up others' violence and downplayed his own   / was believed by experts meant to see through *distorted thinking* to intent to follow through.

What was not taken enough heed of   was written by (two women) forensic psychologists. What was not accounted for was a longer history   that was not properly passed on   call it
Misprison. I first learned that word in a Shakespeare sonnet I memorised at school / It means mistakenness, to have something wrong / Come home again on better judgement making / Misprison of power; misprison of meanings, effects of this event; misprison of history[31]

We cannot survive in this state. Origin story of splitting / of being forced to choose a side   of becoming fixed

This is a lament after the fact of violence. For we all continue to lose.

Doubt at the source puts us beside ourselves: there is splitting. There is something wrong inside. Inside is where the wrong happens. Violence as a drug. Addiction to violent ideology might be   an equal and opposite   reaction to a racist shame   imposed on being forced to choose / or schooled a certain way. I read: cultural erasure is a terror, locked in form. The harms of the atro-city are buried deep   in the lines of the text.   Brutalised, internalised, and returned again to manifest in writing

She is not brought up to hate; she is brought up within the circumference of white language and metaphor, a space that looks and feels to her like freedom: to write this, her only ever attempt at the genre, to risk the (*postcolonial*) fragmented essay   as *immigrant (re) bildungsroman*   or in horror   as his   knives worn as hands, and Jack and Saskia   and all of the   beautiful lives destroyed.[32]

METAPHORS FOR SHAME

How can you understand what you're capable of unless there is someone to show you the way? How can you avoid what might come? *Could you survive as the liar, living in the formal network of the lie?*

There is a void at the heart of the atro-city: it opens wide at school. A part of its depths holds the damage done by the British Empire, the Partition of India. *Kashmir.*

To hold Partition as your history is to live in the conditional tense, as still experienced quietly in object memory (that necklace, that dowry chest, that vase) and also in fiction, in silence and in dreams. In photographs of the dead. It lies still in United Nations' archives, alive in the fate of 8 million people, and in the deadly trade of drugs and weapons pointed across a porous border traced through a river, where the flowing water is no man's land, not story or memory. *Kashmir.*

Though you know *identity as a construct*   it is England in
the early 1980s. There are tales you have heard in another
tongue, though no one in school will teach you. They do not
fit *the narrative*. Your place in this split world is between. This
mother-father language of honour and shame in a country in
denial of its role in your making; you, a child, don't even know
what you're seeking or missing or what you could be with that
confidence of knowledge, the secret your angel-haired friends
live brilliantly inside   unaware they are the custodians

Testify now that to rise in England we must learn   to drown
out the sounds of our mothers' countries, to silence their
courage and read it as shame. Deny their memories of land
/ and water   escape their flat-hand scolding, their insistent
songs   deep code of our DNA. Schooled in a system that
offers no origin beyond the moment our parents arrived in
England, fully formed: grasping on to the old ways still   their
heritage is submerged. Coming up from the wreck as bedtime
stories told or swallowed in food pressed between the deep *life*
lines on their worn hands; there is a voiding of our stories   of
our true formation of   joy we might hear at home   it is
truncated, elided, language silenced, every moment forces us
to choose: as culture curates our disappearance   and what is
the price of that?   And where will it end? Ask the questions
again. Dark woman, again, again, in fragments, and in lament
(and after Gertrude Stein,) *What is it that history teaches*? *History
teaches*[33]

In the atro-city do they teach that after empire   hundreds of thousands of   categories from former British colonies were *invited*, as they say, to fill a labour shortage and help rebuild and care for the UK after World War II? The *Commonwealth* was the term before it gave way to *immigration*. It does not teach the children but learns them well: all their different and varied and multiple beloved lives will form inside the unbending architecture. Next game of empire: to build one again at home.

In the atro-city, we are schooled that Black and brown youth have no history but are lucky to be born in England. That a Muslim boy or a girl is a body of terror. That a Black man must be waiting to attack: must be subject on the street. That a brown girl mute is the best she can be. That a Black girl drowning is a tragic *accident*   her hijab

British South Asians born (of many faiths and none), growing up in post-industrial cities. Sent to seek family honour, self-esteem via success in school – *only connect* – learn that, learn it well. So empire's history, the fullness of it, the schism of it perpetrated by the country that we were born in – goes untaught and so un-mourned – reaction to shame, our ancestors only seen as a monolithic dark mass now living   under surveillance's *eye*   uncivilised so no need to grieve them (even in a pandemic, even now) – the subject even debated as worthy of public attention (as those who served in the British armed forces of World War II, are rarely honoured without some *campaign*,) in mainstream British life.

Instead to survive   a certain way of being and becoming remember *the first lesson of passing is to do well at school*   to aspire *above all* to an *education* before meeting the reality   in the dominant narrative there

School, which Maria Tumarkin writes, is not school: it is a *metaphor for shame*.[34]

Shame is a bone-deep worm, fed with a deep-vein drug. It is racism as *the icy feeling* writes Bhanu Kapil in *Schizophrene*. Shame is put in us, put on us, brown bodies, dark hair; we are baptised in it then held under, commanded to be grateful for any helping hand. The pervasive fiction that Empire is something to give thanks for – that we should be grateful to be born in Britain, that gratitude is the best we can live for – live with this and grow despite it – the *passing* it demands. Not all of us will survive

I recall living in the heart of the citadel, where I first read Kapil's words. From *Fourteen notes on race and creative writing, (with bonus trauma loop)*: *Do you ever have the feeling a group of white people could kill you, if they wanted to?*[35] There are forms of exclusion and   inclusion that do deep and lasting damage the writer   the poet of colour   sounds the constant warning as *lament*

Who will gather and hold these fragments? Who will, O who will?

These are the options before you: *repeat after me*
High, lauded achievement / everyday assimilation / prison /
All options require a death.

In *Axiomatic*, Tumarkin reminds us to *never discount shame's power, or its cockroach like tendency for lingering on.*[36] (The cockroach infestations in prison cells are not a metaphor)

There are victims and victims and victims in this sentence. He wore that as his armour. Used these arguments to sustain (and so undermine me now as)   Pride in his fiction leaking out through the cracks. We do not use words like *fragile* here. Except for the ego, shattered or ascending. Masculinity: a fiction to itself, seeking a path to its own version of glory. There was an underlying condition. Silence and social life. A form of *segregation*. Story telling. Military men will recognise the promise of belonging, the safety in training: the burning desire to prove: the brotherhood. Against a sense of being disappeared, and a way back to a promised land that no one but he could manifest. He could not hold himself whole to himself. Or: he always could. Opposing ideologies the crowning drugs, flooding the monstrous kingdom of the mind. Addiction is not only a question of self-will. Traces of cocaine were found in his beard hair in the aftermath.[37] Power through the telling of stories   to whoever would listen   mirroring whoever he needed to get his way   while gaining respect as a *convincing fake*

And all the while the extreme ideology / pushing twisted community, predicated on annihilation for its own ascendance. The step from that to violence is your own to make.

None of this is an unknown unknown. But perhaps it is known and not deeply understood enough to change policy, move towards root safety. In *The Muslims Are Coming!* Arun Kundnani writes that official thinking on extremism assumes that flawed structures of identity are the problem, that

> *A void is imagined to exist among white, working class young people where a positive sense of national identity ought to be; a lack of identification with Britishness is supposed to be equally destructive of the proper integration of young Muslims. The absence of an appropriate sense of identity creates an opening for the extremist mindset to fill the void.* [38]

This is a warning from the jagged edge: the void is far deeper, far older than 'official thinking' will admit: the state definition of the 'flawed structure' is deeply flawed itself. It suggests that the disenfranchisement from 'Britishness' lies in the strength and refusal of the *other*   culture (in this case *being Muslim*) to bend to the nation that is the better way. It positions the state as benign patriarch, waiting to embrace the lost. And what is

'Britishness' here? It is this concept and its borders   that need critical attention now, and the *flawed structure*   of the atro-city it constantly makes and remakes.

Meanwhile, Kundnani notes that in some minds,

> *Part of the blame lies in excessive multiculturalism, which supposedly encourages the value of different cultures while not endorsing the majority identity. The answer accordingly is to revive national belonging by defining it in terms of the shared liberal values from which both Muslims and the white working class are currently seen as alienated. On this view, the liberal state positions itself as a neutral mediator…*[39]

The sense of this *multiculturalism* still does not change the idea of the established centre. The absolute whole. The lie of this positioning of the liberal state   *neutrality*   the wreck of it. New forms must be made. Some days this can feel   as impossible   as hope

As educator / philosopher Paulo Freire writes,

> *The solution is not to 'integrate' them into the structure of oppression, but to transform the structure so that they can become 'beings for themselves.' Such transformation, of course, would undermine the oppressors' purposes.*[40]

And let us only recognise the oppressors exist   on two sides, as action and reaction

Unless *transformation* means (as metaphor) to burn the city down

Unless the form is what we mean when we say *decolonise* for   equality of humanness, of culture, of language and

To construct forms of identification which grow from a shared knowledge and acknowledgement of our linked, unequal histories   is to address the core issue, and interrogate this: *Terrorism is not the product of radical politics it is a symptom of political impotence.*[41]

In the immediate aftermath, I think about that, and the finality of his act. Which took dear life, and erased for a time any right or even possibility I felt to say *radical* as a term of something in service to racial justice, towards something   as necessary *to fight for* as good. I lost my way and was looking to   find a route back to the *many* who are attempting to heal   inside.

The flip side of shame is dignity: it is hard to come by, hard to sustain anywhere in the atro–city, this prison of narrative and counternarrative

This complex grief. In the chain of language   I reaffirm the deeper channels that send young men of colour to prison. Not to let this terror shatter the work still to do. I returned to the buried stories of *back in the day*, to reset my compass, to remember the struggle that has come before. As the English school system worked to isolate, and *divide and rule*   brown bodies from each other, a policy that unofficially borrowed an American term: *bussing* and made it something else.

Bussing in England was about immigration, integration or assimilation and deficiency in English […] in the United States it was about desegregation and the righting of a historical wrong for African Americans who to state the obvious, […] were not immigrants.

In England, to deal with those categories of working class people and the   threat they posed

many thousands of Asian pupils were forcefully transported to faraway schools, especially in Ealing and Bradford […] their parents had little or no say in it, or did not know they could have a say, and most of those children were of primary school age…[42]

These practices morph via chains of connection: the English language loves its reflective echo as narcissus of pain. *What does a language retain of the violence it has been used to commit?*[43] In the UK the policy was officially referred to as *dispersal*, the word also used in high-security prison, for *terrorists* moved around the country's prison estate, high risk dispersed among low. It is meant to keep *terrorists* from radicalising others, (it does not work). Would it put them in training   always to make new tribes, wherever they land, as becoming part of a gang, even becoming the leader?

Creating new stories of old histories, where that might be the only way to sustain?   The state solution is

   Segregation. Which is another way of saying *exclusion / isolation* as Black working class boys were once *funnelled out of mainstream school and sent to schools for the 'educationally subnormal' (ESN)*, as they are now disproportionately sent to Pupil Referral Units (PRUs) and *excluded* from school as a form of social curation, as Bernard Coard wrote in 1971: *a low self image, and consequently low expectations in life … are obtained through streaming, banding, bussing, ESN schools, racialised news media, and white middle class curriculum; by totally ignoring a black child's language, history culture and identity.*[44] A 1988 CRE Report entitled Learning in Terror insists on how shockingly routine racial bullying, racist violence and name-calling were in British playgrounds.[45] And a 2020 report finds that *for the last forty years the state has responded to inner-city youth rebellions and political agitation for racial and social justice by depriving working-class communities of education.*[46]

There is a reason it is called the school-to-prison pipeline, the PRU-to-prison pipeline, the prison-industrial complex. There is a language and history and policy and schooling for churning out occupants for ever-expanding cells

The *terrorist* had this in his story; left school at fourteen and no one remembers why or how and no one made him go back. He went to prison and came out   *more high risk   than when he went in*

I breathe out. Jack did his master's degree in Criminology at Cambridge. Though it was not so widely reported in the media, the title of his thesis was *The Over-representation of Black, Asian and Ethnic Minority Men in the UK's Criminal Justice System*. As of March 2020, 27 per cent of prisoners were from a BME background, compared with only 13 per cent of the general population. Muslims now make up 12 per cent of the prison population in England and Wales.[47] People who identify as Black comprise only 3 per cent of the general population but 13 per cent of adult prisoners.[48] Young Black adults are: twice as likely to receive a caution, 8.4 times more likely to receive a conviction, 1.5 times more likely to be sent to prison, given prison sentences that are 80 per cent longer than those given to white young adults who commit similar offences.[49]

Then gangs and radicalization inside mirror the landscape and intensify   *There is a real risk of a self-fulfilling prophecy: that the prison experience will create or entrench alienation and disaffection, so that prisons release into the community young men who are more likely to offend, or even embrace extremism*, report after report concludes.[50]

In the UK, 90 per cent of incarcerated adults in Britain never finished school; 70 per cent of incarcerated youth never finished school. What about the young men who are embraced by extremism, and are sent to prison as *finishing school*?

I don't think children are born good or evil. Just into a certain world. And what are they to do?

> If our prison population
> reflected the make-up
> of England and Wales,
> we would have over 9,000
> fewer people in prison.
> The equivalent of twelve
> average-sized prisons. [51]

This is a series of facts *deranged*. The word has its origin late 18th century: from French *déranger*, from Old French *desrengier*, literally to disperse, to 'move from orderly rows'. Here I am, as Hecuba trapped in Dante's *Inferno*, moving words, moving lines; wild with grief to the point of moral despair. *Deranged, she barked like a dog: so far had anguish twisted her mind.*

Second and third and fourth generation children can no longer sustain the mainstream myth of our parents' arrival or our own birth as our only legitimate point of origin. That we have no documented history, that we struggle towards the bright goal of assimilation devoid of state's harms, that the void can be filled later as restorative justice, as   rehabilitation when there was never genuine habilitation   for minds born and raised as unhomed as unhinged that there is no malign power in such a world but we make it. These relentless fictions terrify me   and what they might produce

Heart broken in the extreme duality of the world that raised
me   that raised
the unforgivable hand
that chose to hold the knife – I will say this

    I must lament: world, hand, knife.

    I must do this, even if alone.

    How can I otherwise hope to make anything better to
come?

    Come with me, mother, sister, friend. Come with me, fear
and grief.

This is not to say why, only visit *how*. There is a sweet, whole
life to be had. There is love to find. And there is cold, deep,
fear. I turn again to the mermaid, diving into the wreck   to
read with *you*

We are, I am, you are
by cowardice or courage
the one who find our way
back to this scene
carrying a knife, a camera
a book of myths
in which
our names do not appear.[52]

If we cannot name ourselves and each other   in the sense of
our shared histories, we cannot find solace in our own skins,

or make any kinship across relentless divides   that might demolish the atro-city, that structure that constantly denies it fails us   in which our hopes to live still flare.

BEFORE AND AFTER

In the days of the immediate aftermath, I could not sleep. All I wanted was to go back to the day before. If nothing else, to tell Jack *do not go to London tomorrow*. And further back – who knows how far?

Thursday, 28 November, 2019: A full, busy day. You and Jack are working together inside the prison. Jack is hosting a workshop on the life and teachings of Malcolm X, led by visiting UCLA professor Bryonn Bain. Your writing students join in with a larger group. You remember it as a day of laughter, shared stories: electric with effort. There is a reunion of sorts. For you with men you haven't seen for a year, two years: you are glad to meet again. Their children have grown older, they say.

In the late afternoon, your small group of writers from university and prison leaves the larger space for their final seminar of 2019. You end the day on a bittersweet note: finalising the drafts of pieces they have been working on through the semester. You leave full of plans for the next meeting, which will take place in January 2020, after the winter break. It is hard to leave. Yes, when we share stories with those who must stay, prison is hard to leave.

Friday, 29 November, 2019: You do not go to the gathering at Fishmongers' Hall, though you have been invited. You stay at home and prepare notes to chair an admired writer at a literary festival event, taking place in two days' time. In this life, your other, public, literary life, fictions of self are heavily curated. In some ways this splitting is an act of protection for those who spend more time alone creating others' speech. But perhaps it asks something specific also of writers with immigrant histories, who – though skilled in navigating and code switching in mainstream life – might have so much further to travel, when focus on our work puts us in the public gaze. Perhaps it can feel like a performance of the oldest pattern repeating, as a *trigger*, as it is called

Saturday, 30 November: the bright day. You are at home. *Objective correlative*: Hot coffee and fresh pastries. Breakfast with a friend; your partner in the other room, winter sun coming in through the skylight, the door is open, the coloured glass reflects and refracts, and you see him scrolling, reading something on his phone. He says, *Learning Together.* He says the perpetrator's name

A sensation – like floating – while feeling the hardness of the chair you are sitting on digging into your back. Your phone is next to you: you text *Please let me know you and the team are physically OK when you can*. You remember stepping outside to the sharp incongruity of a world gone white for the first time that year. Trying to de-ice your car: it was parked in the looping street near your house, it would not start.

It is a perfect blue-sky Cambridge day. A frozen day.

When the call came, I remember it as ice, splintering. The shards held in place by the space in between as *cold dark matter*[53], as if the world has become all the absurd facts of an exploded shed by the artist Cornelia Parker, as if even now, metaphor will not be stopped. Even while I write, I am enraged by language, can only turn once again to lament

Who will gather and hold these fragments? Who will, O who will?

One shard is caught in the tight folding arms of individual kindness and institutional violence. The same College people who offer tea and biscuits and to talk in the chapel and walks along the river and hugs in the office and call late at night – wonder if from now on, *anyone* who has *any* association with prison, or a criminal record at *any* level *in the whole university*, should be made to declare it, and banned from coming into contact with students *at all*. You think this sounds crazed (or

is it you?) as you realise the limits of this imagination   what
about the Cambridge students who might have   family
members inside   The adults with long histories who have
earned a second chance (now maybe academics / supervisors
/ administrators in the College office / heroes of the kitchen
/ the servers and the cleaners of some place like this)   the
ramifications of *such policy* make you catch your breath   As
in asides to others (but so you hear) they wonder if *you*, in your
position (which is granted as gift), *deserve* official support now.

You sit in fine rooms and are asked questions that (though
a closed meeting of the College Council had approved the
scheme, though many have praised its effect on the students) in
three years you have never been asked.

How dangerous are the men? It is a high-security prison. I do not
know offending history, although I have asked and asked. I was
told to google

How were they selected for the course? By the prison and LT
management

How are they monitored in the room? In the first year there is a
guard behind a podium, in the second and third years there is a
table for them, at a remove from the class. There are two guards
and sometimes there is only one. There are body searches,
cameras

How safe are the university students when they come into contact

The phrase sends your mind to parabola, not as dance but vortex. To the times you raised these same questions with your *line manager* and talked about the vulnerability of the writing room. The way you designed your course   became to mitigate that   *risk*   in the absence of any other guidance   and your history of youth work made you determined to protect them from   the crossing of lines   as much as you only could. As they *come into contact with*   professors in tweed jackets as year after year, told in stories from *Oleanna* to *Disgrace*   as they are taught to *trust the police*   who harm   do not respect women's harm   race harm   as *Criminals do not always come tagged*, you think *but this is a different set of conditions*. This was a *guarded* man who had been in high-security *prison*   he was already known   *the highest risk*. He was admitted to your classroom and   was *released* for what he then went on to *do*

It does not occur to you until months have passed and your shock begins to clear, to ask them why they do not already have this information. At that moment all you can wonder is if the other teachers are sitting in identical rooms being processed in this way. Later you will read the poet Wendy Trevino and this will strike your mind as something apprehended years ago, when you were starting out. *Institutions that position individuals to reinforce racial hierarchies will always be inhumane, regardless of the individuals who work for them.*[54] You are here, now learning this again, and again, as if you hadn't learned it hard enough, back then, back then and then and then   the abdication by power onto   as they ask again

How could you bring shame   how could you   hold onto this work did it not bring joy?

Disenfranchised grief becomes splintering doubt   invites you into that old feeling   *shhh*. The one-way currency of the atro-city   you are primed to receive it, and to pay.

I never forget I am writing in the wreck.   Around a *terrorist* full of his own hateful narratives, who killed those who cared to make space for him to learn.   To teach him and not know that he violently bullied and radicalised men in prison; was known on the wing for this, including, it is reported months later, persuading one who attacked guards in the aftermath, in Britain's first terrorist attack to take place inside.[55] He was a liar, obsessed with status and ideology. He had no concept of his own risk. *We are talking about public safety*. After his release, months before the event, there was a chance for the University to know his offending history inside prison: it was not taken. He was invited back to Whitemoor by them for a symposium on digital education inside. He met *important people* and was well received. He told former wingmates he was planning an attack. He told a visitor who came to his home that he was writing a play. Called *Drive North*, it was about a terrorist who commits knife crime. I never saw it, or any such violent work. MI5 did. They called it *rehabilitative* and passed it down the chain to police. Who did not pass it on[56]

You are shattered and still leaving the house. Propelled by your training to mask any damage that only those who have lived this (or are forensic psychologists) might recognise. Did you recognise it, *as dangerous compliance* in him?   You keep going in circles, if only to keep going, as if dissembling for your own survival. *This grave and awkward mask*

While in another hour you will be sitting across the hall and up the ancient staircase, in a turret office. Listening and sharing time and words with the small band of students who were inside the prison with you and Jack just two days before. There are apples on the coffee table. They take one each as they leave.

Who will gather and hold these fragments? Who will, O who will?

Sunday, 1 December. Shock makes it seem even more important to stay focussed on the task of chairing that literary event – as if survival could be based on trying to stay in a life that anyone is only ever a guest in, only ever passing through

In the green room, you greet the guest writer. There is a sense of disassociation rising as she asks you if you teach here: you swallow your confession down your throat. You run   you ran the prison-writing programme   and *Jack is dead*.

She has come to talk about her life and her art. The relationship of those things to each other. You walk through the gates, through the courts of a College and in the hallowed hush: there are the rooms where you as an undergraduate wrote papers on St Augustine's *City of God* and on *Confessions*, where you smoked student weed, and had student sex when you were 20, writing fiction in secret. You see yourself fleetingly through the window, putting pink ribbons and butterfly clips in your hair on graduation day, the bright, hot summer of 1999, knowing you would be *asked* to take them out again, unknowing everything to come.

Now *Jack* and *Saskia* are dead. In single file, you and a group of festival people walk behind the guest writer over the beautiful, covered Bridge of Sighs, named after the bridge in Venice, so resonant for its prisoners. Do you believe this occurred to you then? All I can say is, it did. By lucky timing another writer is on the other side of the bridge, they are someone your guest knows beyond the moniker. Each greets the other ecstatically. Everyone else forms a circle, respectfully. You swallow the choking words in your throat, and you realise you should not be here in the court. You knew this when you were here as enraptured and angry, determined and young, lit with the audacity of your parents' belief in you, call it hope, some days call it expectations. Before you became aware that you were cast in the shame of your race and gender and bowed with your body and its history of obedience: tokenism as class-based disease, doubled up with the affliction of gratitude as the *price of the ticket.*[57] Years have gone by – the stones are the same only even more worn.

And though you now know that this feeling is nothing but an infestation of white fictions, constructed to hold you and indoctrinate you as the cathedral arches around you: right now the sickness is winning. Your body feels like a stain, a bruise, full of hair, enormous. You should not be going on stage. You cannot move, you want to punch at the stone façade, you want to die for it and because of it: you want to disappear. You separate from yourself / and also cannot escape   Every doubt from every age comes shrieking through the arches

Thirty seconds pass.

You are expected to be good, to be clever, to be quiet. To be *so articulate* and what is a prison to most people? A metaphor for something. The body is the first prison – the image is the rest. Especially here in this hallowed space, especially now, when to make a sound would be to end everything/ change nothing, and you think you seem absolutely fine   because no one has stopped you yet   while *Jack and Saskia are dead, and the other, his armoured body   and yours*

'Behind bars' actually refers to a cage. To many, prison means for life.

You kept walking to the auditorium. Habit and adrenaline chaired the event. Even now, you cannot remember a single second of it. Time begins again as you come off the stage and are caught by a friend, who later says that your face in that moment was ashen: brown, turned grey. You left the college through the back-gate and went to the nearest pub – it happened to be The Punter, where Jack once worked. You drank a glass of red wine.

Afterwards, walking home alone along the main road in the winter's early dark, cars sped past you: you broke down in the street. Making some kind of noise. A corduroyed woman on an upright bicycle with a bunch of bananas in her wicker basket stopped beside you. She asked if there was someone waiting for you inside. She said she had cried in public like that herself. Then she cycled away.

Monday, 2 December – almost immediately, the media arrives on colleagues' doorsteps and at their places of work; stories are already being written about this, all over the world, new threads in the global narrative of *Islamist, terrorism, surveillance, stop and search. Prison expansion, harsher sentencing, rehabilitation impossible, education naïve, heroes, evil, intention. Life-changing scheme.*

Jack's family, his girlfriend, friends and colleagues gather in the Market Square. Some of those from the University also come to pay their respects, and people from around town. A similar gathering for Saskia on the campus where she studied. Our heads down, the only noises are made by press photographers, climbing on bins and clinging to posts to get a better angle;

and then the sound of people quietly grieving, camera shutters clicking a thousand beats per minute, like hundreds of pieces of soft paper, tearing. It is December, but there is warmth as people move together in the crowd.

You cannot speak for the choking sensation you now live with. Then two separate journalists from the same national newspaper email you. They send their condolences and invite you to offer words about Jack for pieces they are writing – separately? together? They appear not to know about each other, though they both spell and construct your name wrong in exactly the same way. You think about the demographics of their office, and the staff who inputted your name into databases. It is a paper you've written for, in which your fiction – that other life – has been written about: they don't make the connection. For once it is uncomplicated: you are *grateful* for their error. You do not reply.

Tuesday, 3 December – Now come more calls from College high-ups, for walks along the river, to 'talk' as if to share. While also asking for emails, paper trails, traces, publications, you are advised not to speak, in person, in print or in any virtual avatar to media *for protection* – call it fear of tarnishing a world-leading reputation, offending donors, the *Daily Mail* – the institution has five centuries of experience in self-preservation: the people who administer it comply, their compassion vocal, but underwritten. Our lives and minds pass through it: to survive it our voices must sing the same hymns. Doubled over with the shock that follows *terror*, compounded by these words. Charged to preserve the structure of power – silence is the demand, the punishment and the reward. There are things we think we cannot risk to say.

Lorde writes that our silence will not protect us. Sara Ahmed responds: *it could protect them. And by them I mean: those who are violent, or who benefit in some way from silence about violence.*[58] The prison.

I take a breath, I write: now you go deeper into the wild, surreal: the experience of breathing enters a new literary genre. This is surely fiction   *as paranoia*   when you *confess* that the men you taught in his year have a copy of your first novel. There is some speculation that a tenacious right-wing journalist, one who *also knows who you are* as a *writer*, might *think that you* have been *radicalising* in prison with your *fiction* against Indian fascism. The novel was published as you began to teach inside; the men in your writing class read the reviews: proud of the good and joking with prison humour over the bad (*we know where that critic lives*). They had cheered you through. They requested copies to mark the course finished. It contains a critique of state sanctioned violence: Hindu settler-colonialism in Kashmir.

You unfold a map in your mind and see the tear-here perforation of the 'line of control' between India and Pakistan. For all the decades of your life plus all the decades of his, Kashmiris have been subject to legislation inherited from the British that now allows state impunity against the majority Muslim population there. Torture, disappearances, rapes, boys with stones shot by army gun pellets that blind: disappeared and murdered youth, half widows you have met, torture centres, the sweeping away of constitutional protections as you wrote it in the novel in 2017, the rubbing out of the right to self-determination which came, in reality two years later, in the August of 2019 and treated as world surprise. Then more violence, more sanctions, surveillance, deprivation

An accurate description runs the risk of sounding like hyperbole.[59]

He was sentenced for planning a jihadi training camp there, or was it Pakistan. He told his prison probation officer that Kashmir *was* an issue   He told someone he talked to often that it was not. And went to London   and now I am here, preparing to respond to the notion   that my *novel*   might fuel a hate like that

You think of the void so carefully curated, protected and tended to. The history elided, colonial culture lauded, the lectures undelivered, the stories determinedly unpublished, untaught. You think of the misnamed emails from the press;   *would that reporter also know   of the distinction   of fiction and fictional geography made real by the LoC*   between *the territory* of your *novel and* Pakistan-administered / Azad Kashmir?   And its vast district, a city, an everyday place – Mirpur   Would they be careful and not place him in *representation*   knowing that almost a million Pakistanis in Britain come from there. Would they know how they came 'over here?'

It is a story for school children everywhere; as South Asia's history flows into the West's; as wealth is meant to be common, as in *abundant* and so *shared.*   It is a story of the political, social and economic control that causes a climate to change. It is a story of land and sea   and *human life*   it involves kinship networks established in the 1940s, when Mirpuris were enlisted onto British merchant navy ships, and landed in England and settled to work. It continues with Partition: the sectioning off by the Radcliff Line of water resources between two *new* countries, leaving Pakistan in danger of becoming parched. It precipitates the construction, in Mirpur, of the vast Mangla Dam, designed in the 1960s by the English firm BINNIE AND PARTNERS (who would also serve as lead engineers and inspectors), it was constructed by a consortium of eight American companies, based in San Francisco. While the balance required the submergence, say *drowning* of 280 villages, the displacement of 110,000 rural *Azad Kashmiri / Pakistani / Mirpuri* people from their ancestral homelands[60] at the very moment when there was an English need for cheap labour at home in steel, in textiles, in engineering all across the Midlands, including his town, Stoke on Trent.[61] Then comes an industrialist's investment from Britain – the sponsorship of visas – for a certain class of workers – the promise of another life – as *Immigration controls and culture curates*[62] and welcomes all new arrivals to the spiced rhetoric of *Rivers of Blood*[63]

Let the poet speak instead. Of *Kashmir* trauma-looped by the LoC. Let the work of Agha Shahid Ali – who wrote of that place as *The Country Without a Post Office;* who knew it as *a prison,* as Palestine also is – be taught in England's schools. The canonical *revolutionary poets* themselves love their country while they hate   the boundaries of the nation, as they leave it to *its madness and its weather,* and they say   that *poetry makes nothing happen*[64] – so now (as GCSE exam question) – what would the risk be of that?

> … *It's raining as I write this. I have no prayer.*
> *It's just a shout, held in, It's Us! It's Us!*
> *whose letters are cries that break like bodies*
> *in prisons. Now each night in the minaret*
> *I guide myself up the steps. Mad silhouette,*
> *I throw paisleys to clouds. The lost are like this:*
> *They bribe the air for dawn, this their dark purpose.*
> *But there's no sun here. There is no sun here.*
>
> *Then be pitiless you whom I could not save—*
> *Send your cries to me, if only in this way:*
> *I've found a prisoner's letters to a lover—*
> *One begins: "These words may never reach you."*
> *Another ends: "The skin dissolves in dew*
> *without your touch." And I want to answer:*

I want to live forever. What else can I say?
It rains as I write this. Mad heart, be brave.[65]

Let us teach Ali not only for the sake of metaphor. But to reverse the narrative of *the flood*. Remembering that whatever happens, poetry *survives*

In the valley of its making where executives
Would never want to tamper, flows on south
From ranches of isolation and the busy griefs,
Raw towns that we believe and die in; it survives,
A way of happening, a mouth.[66]

Let us hear the implications of our silence. Not to say (outrageously) that *there are no innocents*, but to break what Wole Soyinka calls the *climate of fear*[67]   And for the sake of asking   *who knows, who holds any of this history across our oceans? Who will it pass to next?*

To hear, without this history, that *homegrown* British *terrorists* plan to build training camps in Pakistan/ Azad Kashmir/ Kashmir, is to be invited to imagine *a monstrous other − a monster who is not quite human like the rest of us, who is capable of extraordinary harm and incapable of pain but does not feel it as we do, a monster we and our children must be protected from at any price.*[68] It is *terror* they mean, as an event that happens   across the world and near as it reaches us

This is not to underestimate the criminal immensity[69] of the actual case. Instead, as citizen, to claim the right to appeal —

Not to drive the nation deeper into an isolationist monologue / a defiant unilateralism that appears to thrive on hysteria and deception

(as Soyinka wrote about America   after September 11, 2001.)[70]

While all your learning teaches you that a sovereign state will continue to protect its precious voids; will dig them deeper, as trenches, as entrenched   as the waterline rises, flooding grief on grief, you know, meanwhile, along with Roy that *a shadow world is creeping up on us in broad daylight.* Monstrosity as global fascism. It flows from India, from America, from Britain; it powers *Hindus for Trump,* funded by billionaires in the diaspora, it supports genocidal Modism, which the UK's most senior right-wing politicians tacitly, with trade and policy and other political kinship networks endorse. All linked through a deep, mythologically driven Islamophobia, embraced through class harms: digital platforms, voter ID cards and immigration rules that will spare no one, from 12-year-old Shukri Abdi standing on a river bank,[71] to Shamima Begum, groomed into ISIS then consigned to statelessness, and the men who buy into an alternative promise of power, the violent ideology, extreme drug, who will use this *as their rationale*   you have lost any tongue   in the aftermath   to talk of this out loud.

Mad heart, be brave. If I sound angry it is because I am grieving. If I am grieving it is because   I have been living in these silences for years before I began breathing. Sound anger, and no one will listen. Let us at least lament that.

In the cold College office, again you are *encouraged* not to speak. Instead you are presented with a list of possible questions the media might ask you, regarding your *novel* in relation to the *terrorist*; you must practice the appropriate, pre-scribed replies. While the course convenors names and the creative writing seminars are archived from University websites and kept from the press.[72]

You walk from that office down the concrete border paths. Through the sunken winter beauty of the College courts. You leave through the back gate. You cross Jesus Green, going slowly despite the cold. You consider the phrase *damage control*. You think about heartbreak, and about the real work it takes to make a high-security prison more liveable, knowing that could never be enough. You think about the many students who say their lives have been affected   even changed, incrementally through the writing programme and the other courses, sometimes just enough   the prison governor who could not believe the feeling on the wing among those who took part – *it was as if it became a different prison*[73]

There is still a chance of keeping connection   The possibility of doing *something*   a small safety in the maelstrom – a collectivity to find – believing as Gargi Bhattacharya writes, from heartbreak, with heartbreak, that –

Heartbreak is the moment when we see our pain as only a moment in the battle between the will to live and love and the will to destroy

Heartbreak is when we commune with those who have been broken apart by state violence and we understand that this violence is also meant for us

Heartbreak is when we realise that there is no remedy, no repair, no way back and nothing to fix this. That whatever comes next these histories and presents of violence cannot be put right. That the destiny of the heartbroken is to wish something better and completely new for those who come next.

Because it is only we, the heartbroken, *who can truly battle and long for a   world where no-one ever feels like this again.*[74]

I read her words a year after the event. Time allows me some grace. Her construction *we, the heartbroken* opens a moment of clarity, allowing me back into pure grief. It is a call to find in community the sense that there might be a return from the event as shattering of trust. This is the kind of mourning the state does not want us to participate in, that it fears from us.

It also has echoes of Shakespeare's ambivalent last lines in *King Lear*, which we can read as a call to *see better* the harms the state forces us to live within. When I read that play at school, I learned for the first time that the Partition of the subcontinet had a place in the curriculum, even if only as metaphoric representation. I experienced the play as British, as Indian, and woman under patriarchy. I saw power's hubris towards the poor; land divided to a sovereign will, a map, intent on division, the love test a parallel of Imperial divide and rule as policy, it read to me as a call to action for social justice; a trust *in what could be*. My own work was forged in the gap between the assumption of my silence as the right way to be, and wanting to write what I knew.

Writing is living enthrall to radical doubt. About what we might be capable of. As if in the grip of the longing to die and the desire to make revolution: there exists two equal and opposite forces. The friction makes sparks and in the fire – the same place a creative impulse comes from, the same place that real teaching is called from – vocation, incantation, the drive to make something that has not been imagined yet, flawed if it must be formed out of the fragments of what is left, in denial of what was once already there: at heart – from language, from what we teach and are taught, and read.   And on the flip side: who gets to write, and not only that: who is read. Whose art is allowed to be valued for public consumption: who makes the allowance, what the allowance is.

BACKSTORY AS EVENT THAT HAPPENS

Michael Fischer, American, writer, formerly incarcerated, lays it out in a literary magazine:

> *If you've been imprisoned in America and want to write, your story must fit into one of three molds. You can be innocent. You can be a reformed convict who committed a violent offense long ago and spend most of your time emphasizing how sorry you are, how long it's been since you offended, and how much you've changed. Even then, it can be fraught territory; when it comes to violence, no punishment is too long or severe. The third narrative mold is the one I've poured myself into. It is the Golden Goose: sexier and more dangerous than the innocent, more palatable (and publishable) than the violent. I am a "nonviolent offender."*[75]

I walk ten miles along wild coastline one hot summer's day. I think about these words, and the men inside as I met them. The things they had done. Their writing. Of Jack and Saskia. The sense I have of being bound to this event through powerful emotions and a sense of responsibility, even if I was not only accountable alone. Not only through the confluences of history and politics, and proximity   a writer's need to write

I walk across the burning sand to the shoreline; I wade into the sea. I am not seeking rebirth, absolution (if that was mine to seek) – but oblivion, perhaps. Now even the waves seem to pause. Salt water floods into my mouth – a simple sentence forms in my head. Somebody I knew died: somebody I taught killed him.

It is a moment of separation from the terror. A tiny shift, as a muscle moves under water to keep the body afloat. A re-formation. Back towards the logic of context   cause and effect and political responsibility which the violence and its aftermath had split me from

Seven months have passed before I can come to this. *That we can be injured, that others can be injured, that we are subject to death at the whim of another, are all reasons for fear and grief,* Judith Butler says.

Grief hurts enough. I do not want this writing to cause more harm. I know words can be a metaphor for the knife. I perceive this thought as despair. Am I the non-violent offender, writing about the aftermath of the offence? I have done no harm but this: I have brought the body   this fractured text here to you. Remembering that it is just one in the mass of the atro-city.

There are many others, including yours, all bound.

Still, I could not forget that Butler's words were written for the hundreds of thousands of civilians across Iraq, Pakistan, Afghanistan, Syria, Yemen, killed by Western imperialism after that 'event', as originator of all that came after – the US-led, UK-supported *war on terror* – 9/11. In *Precarious Life* Butler also focuses on the detainees denied all human rights or reason, far off in Guantánamo Bay. Would she make space for the brown and Black youth in prison, or the few inside for the very terror that sparks and mirrors, that preys on the structures of the atro-city, on language and on kind hope   and has ended in *these* deaths?

When it comes to *homegrown terror* as murderous violence – when it comes to the deaths of people trying as best they could to make a difference (within the rules of the atro-city) – such as those who work in prison education and arts – even Judith Butler, even *nonviolent offender* Michael Fischer, might pause. My body remains heavy on me, as the oxymoron of *just war*.

I read Kundnani again and remember that

> *The question of terrorist violence carried out by an extremist or ideological non state actors is inseparable from the wider background of state violence that is defined as normal, necessary, and rational.*[76]

The *homegrown terrorist* knew this, said he felt it. Whether or not this was misprison, or somewhat true, he was born British / *other* in the immediate shadow of 9/11, which happens when he is ten years old. 9/11 was not the start: but for many it was.

Where were you on 9/11? Do you remember Algiers, Bradford, Bali, Madrid, Paris, Pittsburgh, Christchurch, Manchester, DC, all the complexity of the lost? *How many websites would we need to pay heed to all the dead?*[77] For some, London on July 7, 2005 (7/7) was the starting point. And this is a definition of trauma. Not the thing itself, but the repetition of the event. No origin story except in the moment of the arrival of death. The aftermath of 7/7 was hammering, punitive for British Muslims, as writers including Sabeena Akhtar, Nesrine Malik, Kundnani, Tawseef Khan (who also speaks of the post traumatic psychological *split*[78]) and Tarek Younis document.[79] Without their words and activism, the true impact of state policies on Muslim lives would remain even further hidden from public view in Britain's national story. They give voice to the ever more complex impact of increasing and constant surveillance which has come about partly because of the framing of 9/11 as a single origin *event* – the beginning – and 7/7 being understood as its British iteration. Their work offers important reckoning with the repeated traumas that the *war on terror* enabled in terms of the widening of the Home Secretary's powers – in policing, counter-terrorism, prison expansion and fuelling of Islamophobic racism in the years since then.

On 7/7 I was living in London. I woke up in my lover's bed and we left his rented room, heading for the tube at Elephant and Castle, with its echoes of imperial ivory trade. He was bound for Kings Cross station, and then to the northeast of England. The tube was closed. We walked the streets to the river, tracing the route of the No.1 bus. We crossed at Southwark Bridge. Up through Bloomsbury, heart of English literary aspiration (and in its green squares, in 1931 the wave seemed to pause, and *then drew out again, sighing like a sleeper whose breath comes and goes unconsciously*,[80] as the current was pulling towards this day. Kings Cross was closed, and we carried on to Highbury and Islington, where we planned to spend a night. The streets were wide and mostly empty in my recall. In London's silence was a sense it had been hoping against   an event that now seemed inevitable. The only sound was sirens.

SEPTEMBER COMES AGAIN

Four years earlier, I was 22 and *freelance*. The word evokes the heroic Romantic, the word evokes exhibitionist violence, its origins in *hired mercenary* – of the great imperial age – nineteenth-century racial capitalism underpinning a clash of civilisations; an epic war. I thought I knew things, and maybe I did, although I didn't know then what they were. By then I had a year's worth of observational training in the ways of the city: a first job as a junior reporter on a *Financial Times* trade paper, covering pensions: could not add two numbers in my head but could pass at advanced level among the whiteness of high finance and the national print press. Then my mother was diagnosed with terminal cancer. I lost all feeling for saving or the future. This ludicrous job now became untenable: I went home to care for her. But I still had the clothes, and the business card. I was ready to make my own way.

I aimed to become a social-affairs or a foreign correspondent, though really to write and publish fiction. I had not yet understood that in the nature of the atro-city these were almost impossible dreams. And then September 11 came.

Every two years at that date, a trade fair takes place at the vast Excel Centre in the heart of London's retro-future empire, Docklands, a *Blade Runner* set in the making, where in the nineteenth century, England's trade ships were built and used to depart and land with goods harvested by and from, the colonised world. The borough is now home to 46.1 per cent working-class British Asians.[81]

The acronym of the fair is DSEI. I, midnight's grandchild, with an early-learned weakness for a hybrid aural pun, rearrange the letters and read DESI instead. But it does not stand for the diaspora, or the word you use about your tribe on the cover of your LGBTQ-zine. Not either for the beautiful brown boy with the muscles and the stubble and the eyelashes in the market or the bank or the doctor's or the dentist's or in the college canteen: see him dreaming of being an actor one day, maybe playing cannibal or Caliban, or the one corruptible civilian, no, make it the weak policeman; or the ma-loving sex-pest, or even leading the show as *an accidental jihadi* in a Brit-flick satire on the world's big screens. Or just a straight up terrorist with a knack for dissembling – he'll take what's given and make it work – if he won't, someone else will. Nor is it the kind of British Asian-Bhangra-Qawal mix you turn up loud when there is no one else home, or twenty years later during a global pandemic when everyone is; as the highest numbers of deaths in the UK are among working class Muslims, British Bangladeshi and Black men, and you play Ty's "So U Want Morre (refix)" on repeat

DSEI. Defence and Security Equipment International. The cousins-in-arms of British high finance and high politics; the murky depths of pension funds bonuses, our future 'safety' apparently here, in this vast hall, a quiet, civilised 'convention'.

It was mid-morning in London; New York was still asleep. I boarded the Docklands Light Railway at Bank (as in, the Bank of England) to Customs House, where the taxes and wages of empire-building were once counted. The DSEI had started; there was a protest outside. I thought I'd try to pitch a feature about it. I wore my city-girl skirt suit.

By the time I arrived it was early afternoon. There was news coming through of something happening in New York. Smart phones were still in the future. Something about planes, attacks, crashing into buildings: nothing I could piece together. I spent a short time in the protest but the reason I had really come was to try to get into the fair.

I got through the outside rope security by flashing my defunct FT (trade paper) business card. To the woman on the registration desk, I insisted I had registered. I told her it was not my fault when she could not find my name. She didn't demur. But she could not let me into the Excel. Then she discovered a problem. For security reasons, delegates could only traverse the event in one direction. There was no way out the way I had come. The convention centre was too vast to go around. I would have to go through it.

On September 11, 2001, escorted by security, I walked through an international arms fair. There were white men in suits. Some military camouflage stood out. I think I remember a scattering of Asian, Middle Eastern and Black men among them. Briefcases, lanyards. Highly polished lace-up shoes. I remember the shoes, even now. The national flags. There were soldiers, some privates, some in decorated uniform. The orders and deals. The missiles and early drones on display. It was so quiet. The weapons seemed to me as big as commercial planes. Here was *capitalism as weapon of mass destruction*.[82] Tended to by buyers and sellers all members of the world's most powerful, legal gangs – private companies and nation states – some of which are on watch-lists for human rights abuses, some of which that year may even have been 'at war' with the fair's host country, Great Britain, which today remains the second biggest exporter of arms in the world.[83]

In New York the towers were already burning.

We know that the ensuing *war on terror* would break the hearts and shatter the minds and take the lives of people, there are the numbers, thousands and hundreds of thousands, repeatedly into millions,[84] or locked to violence with PTSD; clockwise, counterclockwise, ad infinitum, we who live *safely* never think that

one day, by some law of *probability* (perhaps as taught on a prison course) that number will come down to three, and then two

and then
to one
and that one
will be
you.

9/11 focussed the trajectory of my life, as it did for so many
of my Muslim and South Asian friends, even lives lived far,
far away from America, or any of the countries that then bore
the brunt of it. This was the space embodied. Many of us
knew people who died in the towers. Many of us had family
and friends in the countries now immediately targeted and
we were expected to defend ourselves in our workplaces and
colleges, and to choose sides – reaffirming the splitting / the
pressure of childhood   it became a question of proving and
defending ourselves, our communities in ways many of us had
never wanted to, or thought we'd have to. In silence and with
gratitude and in denial we had been able to take our right to
humanity and to individuality for granted. Now we knew we
no longer could. It became the subject of our intellectual and
creative inquiry, our art, jobs we were sent on or made for
ourselves; it defined our partnerships and relationships. Our
conversations with friends. The ending of some of those. We
were often pitched against each other as having to *explain*

In the week after the towers fell, I *freelance* (actually, on work
experience), the only Asian and/or female face on the news desk

(night shift), got my break. I was dispatched to East London, to the Bangladeshi Muslim communities on Brick Lane, to report the views of the Unclejis. The night editor thought they would trust me as they talked it all over, unprotected from racist backlash in the proud back rooms of their restaurants while the barricades went up around the American Embassy in a leafy square on the west side of town, just off Park Lane. I went, I sat with them. I remember having chai. They told me what they feared as defence of their humanity, as separation from the event that had happened. I got my first, and last, news by-line the next day. Sick with my own duplicity, I finished my week but did not return to that office, or to a job on a national news desk, again.

As our experiences of everyday life changed in myriad ways, we became alert to the sense of always being watched. Profiling in airports, in our universities, in hospitals, and in our children's schools as a means to   Prevent, the government's counter terrorism strategy, was introduced in 2011. The main focus was on Al-Qaeda-inspired terrorism, though other types are covered. It concentrates on ideology, not politics. It has a way of seeing   and you could do the opposite. It has a way of manipulating ordinary people   into harm. It has no care for origin stories, I am writing this now and I could not be more anguished if I press the keys harder will any of them break? Be calm, be quiet the atro-city politely *requests* your modest civility.

and when we speak we are afraid
our words will not be heard
nor welcomed
but when we are silent we are still afraid

So it is better to speak
remembering
we were never meant to survive[85]

and that is a creed to write by though to some this picture will be unrecognisable, to others semi-acknowledged and half understood. To many it is now a cumulative force, to respond to only in writing. To *him* it was lived and became his *mask* worn daily, as intimately threatening as walking alone in a city, always in a crowd.

Hollow, I marched against the war. I spent the years afterwards working in NGOs, interviewing and reporting for state-level advocacy on minority rights; on the thousands of Assyrian, Yazidi, and Mandaean refugees[86] fleeing from the destruction of Iraq, the rise of Al Qaeda. Under threat of assimilation or eradication people were forced to leave their ancient homeland and seek shelter in Jordan, Lebanon, Syria, applying for refuge in Sweden, in Australia; scant numbers were granted asylum in the UK. I have taken direct testimony from victims of ISIS in its iterations   I have seen   what ideological violence as action   does to bodies and minds   and now this.

In our lifetimes, *back home*   policy has become even more vengeful, more intrusive and punitive, setting communities on each other. It continues to harm, while it productively fails *to keep the public safe*. Something remains profoundly, almost wilfully unfixed: as brown and Black boys and girls are born and grow and come of age in this forfeit and counterfeit world.

This is not about one person, but many   not one evil   but hundreds   let us call them the planners, the architects, the waiting abusers and preachers, manipulators, metaphor for the laws, the police, the elite institutions of the atro-city. A terrorised mind colludes in its own making; it cannot unmake itself from the outside in. Losing hope, hoping for something to come beyond   it can only eventually choose death, and the form of its own destruction, it can only become   *the destroyer of worlds*

Do you feel safe here?

Those I love, who love me, suffer from the trauma of precarity though some have lived in England for five decades and all our paperwork is legit. They entreat me to stay silent. They have voted all of their lives, and carry their passports with pride. They have contributed to community, they have stayed inside when asked. Now they seek refuge in ritual and in prayer. And build strength in that. While I lost my faith in (almost) everything watching others in community and in action: I find

grace in their rituals, their protests; their repetitions contain
something sublime   which I now am exiled from, can only
bear witness to

I never want another mind to be lost in the space between
two extremes. Or to go on to perpetrate such violent harm.
I refuse to call this dreaming. I want a government of heart,
mind and tongue that does not treat lives as contingent. I want
a neighbour that believes the same.

On September 11, 2018, I took the Amtrak from Washington,
DC, to Baltimore, to present *We That Are Young* at the Writing
Seminars at Johns Hopkins University. It was a singular honour
and a hard won dream to travel for my debut book across the
immensity of a country I had visited once as a child on a
Disneyland holiday but really only been exposed to through
television, films, literature, music. And language: leaking from
imagined American cities, through the chains of capitalist
connection all the way to the inner ears of good Indian girls,
tuning their analogue Sony Walkmans in single bedrooms,
somewhere in small town England. The transatlantic route
remapped, put down, flipped and reversed in lyrical beats, the
SugarHill Gang, Cypress Hill, A Tribe Called Quest. Missy
Elliott.

Sometimes on that trip, begun in the heat of Labor Day
weekend, finished in the delicious chill of New York at
Halloween, I had a sense of the ground breaking all around

me, as an earthquake in a Hollywood disaster film. I perceived the long history and harms of anti-black racism; the hurt of it, the challenge so much more urgent and prominent than in England; it struck me again that my country still has so much to *admit*

I took a taxi from the station: the driver asked me what I was doing in town. I told him – smiling – Uncle, my book, my tour. I remember he asked me – *how often do you write? Have you started the next book yet?*

I laughed and said – *from these questions I can tell you are a writer too –*

His answer was a story. Before the attacks on the Twin Towers, he had been a cab driver in New York. He used to write all the time, in Arabic in big black notebooks. In the days after 9/11 he was detained, as many South Asian Muslim men were, and held for 48 hours, his notebooks seized. After his release, he petitioned to get them back, but the authorities told him he had to wait. They wanted to get the writing translated. Eventually, he was told they had spent thousands of dollars, more than he earned in months or a year, and had found nothing. *I could have told them myself*, he said. *They were children's stories.* He asked for his writing back and but they said that the notebooks – his life's imaginings – had been destroyed. He hadn't been able to bring himself to write again. We promised each other that when I began my second book, he would start as well. He asked, and when I got back to New York, I sent him a signed copy of my novel. For his daughters.

In the early months of 2020, just before England went into its first pandemic lockdown, I moved to a city in the northeast of the country. Summer came: I barely knew anyone, could not meet anyone. The streets were empty. In the long heat, the promise of the sea, the screeching of kittiwakes nesting under the vast steel bridge merged with the sirens of ambulances, racing. The only shop doing business nearby was an allusion: *Fifth Avenue Flowers*

September again. Locked in the tidal pull of sorrow, transmitting only through virtual reality and working on these pages: some days it seemed all knowledge had also fled. Tasting doubt like a sickness every day, as physical as a clenching around my throat, there seemed no respite or place to find solace: not in poetry, in philosophy, in political response or in fiction. A friend speaking from another time zone told me I already had all I needed to write this text. That all I had to do was trust narrative.

This is a trust narrative.

II.

RADICALISING

THOUGHT

My dear, if it is not a city, it is a prison.
If it has a prison, it is a prison. Not a city.

'Faceless,' Tongo Eisen-Martin

POETRY

When I dive into the wreck, it is as a brown-skinned woman with tangles of long, dark hair.

I find the bones of transatlantic ships, rusted pieces of twisted iron: shackles. I find the chains. Their links – the words floating upwards as if from the pages of NourbeSe Philip's' *Zong!* She, born the same year as my mother, as Partition, has been here already, and found the ship's log, mentioning no names but the crew, the rest was *cargo*; the rest were chained. They had no papers, the rest dissolved. I hear the hopeful singing of revolutionary songs, while Saidiya Hartman's question echoes through the depths – *how might we understand mourning when the event has yet to end?*

    I am looking for hope   and I encounter the lost mastheads of East India Company merchant traders (one ship was called *The King Lear*), en route to wheat fields and Mughal treasures. And there is my grandmother's crochet hook. A swordfish pierced upon it. Saffron dissolves. The gods of her mandir float past me. There is my mother as a girl, aged nine, sailing to England for the first time, on the last ship before the closure of the Suez Canal: she learned her English on the way. There are the villages, the landscapes of the drowned, there are hoodies and puffed jackets here. Baby shoes: too worn. Aeons pass. There are Barbie backpacks, mobile phones: there are thousands of Syrian voices among the silver fish, the dead. The lament turns to a language I have always loved, as origin and lost cousin, as song through childhood, as Rumi –

how long can I lament
how long
like a prisoner of grief can I beg for mercy
if I can only recount the story of my life, right out of my body
flames will grow –

I open my mouth – I drown.

I want to believe, still, that *the words are purposes, the words are maps*, but at that time I am talking about, I was still breathing, as the terror caused its shock waves, as the force of institutions took their toll; as a long history of silence as a reaction met the full narrative power of the state, the media and the university. The words that belong here are by Diane di Prima, who will die the night before I write this sentence. Calling with the voices of Black American women, she writes enemy to carceral capitalism. In *Revolutionary Letters*, she calls for the complete demolition of the imperial, racist, system of her country – the USA – well, there were months to go, and she had to die, before I could give myself permission to call on her here.

Rich, di Prima, Morrison, Rankine, hooks, Philips; Black women poets and others who distil scales of violence and degradation into bare lines; who write out of pain to joyful resistance, never giving corner to the individual who harms; but always against the state harm arises from. I reach towards them from the seabed. They rise against the state of prison in their words; true radicals, true revolutionaries, their words which by that same fluke of capitalism that brought me Black American music, and seeking and research skills learned the hard way and at the centre of whiteness, also found me, so far from them. They speak of the splitting of racialized violence and imprisonment; they know the need and how to write it, and they know how and what we must lament. They know rage, and they show love. They know this pain of state violence inflicted until it breaks a heart

And yet my body remained heavy. As grief is a force of gravity. It felt too much to ask the scholars and the poets that they hold even this real terror. They are all either dead, or tired, or with arms full. In the immediate aftermath, I lost my faith in poetry, as possible compass, as chart. In the way that trust now resembled rhetoric.

In *The Price of Wealth, the Cost of Care*, Toni Morrison exhorts her transatlantic kin to remember that as a writer:

My faith in the world of art is intense but not irrational or naïve. Art invites us to take the journey beyond price, beyond costs into bearing witness to the world as it is and as it should be. Art invites us to know beauty and to solicit it from even the most tragic of circumstances. Art reminds us that we belong here. And if we serve, we last.

I had always believed her before.

And Claudia Rankine, in *Citizen* – who seemed to see right into this moment where everywhere I looked I saw with her that –

Your hearts are broken. This is not a secret though there are secrets. And as yet I do not understand how my own sorrow has turned into my brothers' hearts. The hearts of my brothers are broken. If I knew another way to be, I would call up a brother, I would hear myself saying – my brother, dear brother, my dearest brothers, dear heart –[87]

I read and re-read, and I thought about what brotherhood means to her and where its boundary might lie. What the poet gives us is the space to choose. I carried toxic sorrow in my veins and my throat: an unmournable body, clamouring. Rankine is speaking of Black people ancestrally caught in the racism of the US carceral system. Not British South Asian Muslim youth/ *terrorists*, not in America but in my green and pleasant land. Context is everything now. *My brothers are notorious,* Rankine

writes. *They have not been to prison. They have been imprisoned.*[88]
I remember how the poet Tongo Eisen-Martin stood and read
from his book one warm, fall night at San Francisco's Alley
Cat Books:

My dear, if it is not a city, it is a prison.
If it has a prison, it is a prison. Not a city.[89]

I have often turned to the poets and poetics of Black liberation,
seeking the words as maps in a politely hostile place. I know that
this speaks to a lacunae in the culture of England, *O, my unfortunate
country*[90], which is largely deaf to the voices of its 'own'; when we
that are Black, brown, and all iterations of struggling, with scarcity,
struggling for self and community representation, struggle for
solidarity while struggling for separation from acronymity; BAME,
with its aural near-pun *bane*; struggling towards allyship, even as
we recognise and lament the hierarchy of caste (as metaphor) and
as a lived diaspora reality; as we suffer the finesse of the state's
exquisite and specific delineations of pain allocated to us by race,
religion, gender and the colour and shade of our skin.

Would the poets allow that *a terrorist* body was imprisoned by the
city, before it was put in the prison manifest? That the problem
of his mind was made worse by prison, and this manifest on
release? Months later, the expert forensic psychologist will say
that it was so.[91] Now, I whisper this question, and I hear the
refrain: *the knives, the hands, the lie. The intention, the care, the lost.*

In the early weeks after the event, every line of Maya Angelou's *When we come to it* struck resonance for me, but this most of all: *Out of such chaos, such contradictions / We learn that we are neither devils nor devines.*[92] There is no theodicy, she tells us: no mission. The existence of evil does not prove the existence of God: that is the missionary's defence. To found any rehabilitation on such a principle is a fundamental mistake. And while I wanted to trust Angelou's words, all I can say is that even poetry – especially poetry's revolutionary potential, made in concentrated language to which doubleness is intrinsic – which I had always trusted – felt like betrayal then. I turned from the poets, full of doubt. I had no right to lay this complex, shattered body at their feet.

I had yet to come to the words of June Jordan, asking graduating students, after 9/11:

And what shall we do – we who did not die?

What shall we do now? How shall we grieve and cry out loud, and face down despair?

Is there an honourable means to pursue and capture the perpetrators of that atrocity without ourselves becoming terrorists?[93]

Jordan knows that poetry can only raise questions. What she does reject is fundamentalism. What she wants instead is to acknowledge and protect our species in all its different sameness. *Fundamental conflict*, she writes, *has no place in that, from any side*. She wants safety and knows it must come with respectful reckoning by people of different faiths towards each other. A secular political state to harbour and cherish diverse systems. Is it possible? June Jordan asks the question. Then she says, *I don't know the answer to that.*

THEORY

I remember standing in a book-lined room, mid-point in a winding staircase of a fifteenth-century tower, in one corner of a pristine court. There are the careful, planted borders   we cannot cross their pretty lines. To the bright green squares of grass; we cannot walk on them. This is a place: this is a real bricks and mortar place. This borrowed office that became a strange refuge for three weeks that winter, after the event.

I scan the shelves and pull down a book. *Trust and Violence.* The author is Jan Philipp Reemtsma, German, thinker, who has written many books about society and its possibilities, though just three of them have been translated into English.

Reemtsma begins with the deepest question that human violence sounds; the one which *severely tests both the writing of history and what our society knows for certain – how could it have come to this?* He wonders why the question persists, when we continually must face the fact of the violent capacity in us. *Though Auschwitz was without precedent,* he writes, and *Germans were the first to build a city solely for the purpose of murder,* (which seems wrong to me, when I consider the *subculture) we have always known that humans are capable of committing atrocities that leave us speechless.* But calling the Holocaust, the deaths of six million Jewish people in a precision-planned way, *a monstrosity without precedent,* he writes, *does not mean that the individual deeds of its predecessors were not without precedent.* He sees the predecessors of the camp guard, the sadist, the tormentor in ancient Rome, which was built on the backs of slaves and imprisoned peoples, colonised peoples, others. Toni Morrison sees the precedent in transatlantic slavery as she writes in the epigraph for *Beloved, sixty million and more.* To me it has its next manifestation in the colonising violence of the 19th and 20th Century; and the myriad wars over the distribution of resources between peoples, which have caused such displacements since then.

For Reemstma, the question is not – *how do ordinary fathers become murderers?* But instead, *how do murderers become our ordinary fathers*? How do they become our politicians, our parents, our friends, our students, who enter with us into the bond of trust, which forms our intimate and social worlds? Reemstma argues that *the question is torturous because it necessitates in us an excruciating ambivalence* [….] *the existence of a gap between the morality that legitimizes a deed and the morality by which we judge it.*[94] He is talking of the denazification of German life after 1945, the children who had to face the atrocities of their parents, in a moral rupture from the crimes of the past.

If nothing else, in this quiet moment, Reemstma's thinking offered me this possibility: to work through the structures of the atro-city: education, culture, art, theory, politics, practice to find alternative possibilities to our current condition, and so back again to this question: *how has it come to this?* There has been no moral rupture for generation after generation in Britain to address its national(ist) narrative of imperialism, the savagery of its crimes: slavery, Empire and colonialism. For too many, that critical ambivalence has been repressed.

Picking up on a literature and culture that valourises the hero's journey (for Black and brown subjects, assimilation; for prisoners, redemption) while it also thinks more deeply about *catastrophe rather than continuity*, Reemstma says, establishes theoretical models that operate on the belief that there is a certain mystery to be solved. However, *the truth* he writes:

> *Is that* there are no mysteries, *only* mystifications, *either of the contrived kind, such as when we describe something ordinary in an unusual way that causes others to fall into speculation, or of the reflective kind, such as when reality collides with our routines or theories, to an extent we can't ignore, yet fails to dislodge them, so attached have we become. If we fail to grasp the origin of the problem and continue to project mysteries into this world, the world will continue to look back at us in kind. What is mysterious is not the catastrophe but our inability to integrate it into our lives.* We mystify the catastrophe to deliver normality from the burden of constant vexation.[95]

In this case, the kind of integration Reemstma calls for might take too much from us. Violence by states against others is a condition we have come to accept as normal. Violence in certain individuals is planted in us as extreme examples of a norm. But this normalisation cannot be challenged without questioning how and who we trust. Trust is where power truly lives. Not in violence. Not in the deep vein drug

We are bound to trust historical power. The story of the state, of dominant culture, of educational institutions. The very places that inscribe binaries as a way of protecting sovereignty. And when they harm us, they can turn us to look for trust in alternative power. Sometimes to finally harm.

Thinking about mourning and violence in the aftermath of 9/11, Judith Butler, the theorist, calls on Arundhati Roy, the activist-essayist-novelist, identifying Osama bin Laden as *sculpted from the spare rib of a world laid waste by America's foreign policy*.[96] The language deliberately evokes Judeo-Christian creation myths, a play on the three monotheistic religions' idea of Paradise; it evokes the Biblical fall (as traumatised pun). More importantly, a theological human origin-story now lies behind the Event. Through Roy's metaphor Butler identifies the distant boogie man the West enabled, whose presence is now among us as *legion* as some might say – a thought that allows Western policy and culture makers to subject *every* Muslim / *funny tinged*[97] person into becoming a potential violent criminal simply hiding in plain sight. It follows, then, that all must be punished through the everyday practice of being suspect and the emphasis on reporting such violence disproportionately, and even more so when perpetrators are

Muslim.[98] This violence as catastrophe (which it absolutely is) has a ripple effect, serving both the terrorist ideology *and* harmful counter-terrorist practices, and the media empires that amplify the event beyond all other harms. In *I refuse to condemn*, Lowkey reminds us of Paul Howlden's term *threat inflation*, where, according to an expert on terrorism for the British Government, we have a one-in-sixteen-million chance of being near an act of terrorism in the UK.[99] As someone who was in a different kind of proximity to the terrorist, if not to the event itself, I do condemn. My condemnation is both specific and *unreserved*

The tragedy is this: the system is so efficient – so convincing and so lucrative to those perpetrating it – that harm will only continue, raising the pressure, the paranoia, the division, the suspicion; lists can raise the heartrate as repetition. Some people, young people, *will* become the story as the script goes. It will only happen to a very few, and though individual grief is never relative, compared to other kinds of 'ordinary' murders or violent crimes, only affect a very few.

These sleights of language do their own damage. Some incarcerated people on long sentences have been in the wrong place at the wrong time; some have been diagnosed with severe mental health problems. And prison is the only place the state can hold them. We know that an *ordinary* son can also kill.

My anguish was this: in that moment I did not believe even Reemstma's theory, reckoning with the relationship between trust and violence would hold this event in a context. Culture has decided it cannot be so. But even one person who commits violence is one too many   for us to call their actions a singular catastrophe.

The question is – what comes next?

The ground becomes more fragile once again. Like Butler, Reemtsma calls on fiction to test out his ethical thinking. He goes to the poets and playwrights, the novelists. Back to the refracted representation, which I taught and have lost the ability to trust.

For the theorist, fiction is the body cut open for thought. But fiction is my problem here. Produced and reproduced, published and sold on the *free market* inside the atro-city, it is still bound by its rules: demand and supply are a hall of mirrors, reflecting mainly themselves while policy and political rhetoric continue in their way

Reemstma ends his introduction by thinking about Adorno's moral judgement: *all culture and cultural criticism after Auschwitz is garbage.* He notes that the purpose of this statement was to warn us against *answering barbarism with self-barbarisation.* We cannot trust the modernity we have made. The fictions we inherit, are schooled in, our *cult*-ure, as Roy herself, made into a cult figure of the writer as advocate, might break the word down; the stories we make and are enabled to sell in the capitalist world need constant breaking, reconfiguring.

If I had to give this text a beginning, I would say that encountering this familiar thought through Reemstma's wide vision made something briefly shift. It was a small moment, difficult to hold on to. In the months that followed it disappeared and resurfaced along with the waves of trauma and of doubt that caught so many of us in their pull.

But it must have taken root as a creative impulse, which could be translated as the beginning of this writing, as a form of remaking a sense of faith in, and with, a practice. Back then, I, an interloper, was lost in the atro-city as citizen of nowhere, standing with a book called *Trust and Violence* in my hands, falling into the gaps left by the known world, from that tower of high culture in the aftermath, in the wake.

CITIZENSHIP AND POLITICS:
A POSTCOLONIAL STORY

First generation postcolonial novels written for Anglophone readers and published in the West usually contain certain markers. The character list, so you can remember all the names. The family tree, so you can remember who is related to who. The italics for foreign words, though to the characters they are not foreign. The question of arrival must be dealt with – the tribulations of becoming *civilised*. The tropes are twins, doubleness, doubling, splitting; the tropes are puns, the tropes are magic, underpinned by myth   there is usually a glossary at the end to explain the terms

This is not a postcolonial novel, with its magic-realism or mirroring devices, its epic confluences of identity. The real British disease of tokenism has to answer for a coincidence of names that I'd question in any student creative work

My name is Preti and hers is Priti Patel. Though we share a first name hers is more Sanskrit than mine   Priti / Preeti / Preethi and my spelling, Preti (which makes sense to a child learning to spell English phonetically) is derived from the Sanskrit *prīti*, meaning *pleasure, joy, kindness, favor, grace, love* (as the doubling of names in such novels are often signifiers of nature and its opposites)   Preti and Priti were born at opposite ends of the same decade: one in March, one in April. Priti's Ugandan-Indian parents left before the terror of Idi Amin; they briefly settled in the same English county as mine did; then her family moved. We grew up under Margaret Thatcher's long, punitive decades, in neighbouring counties: she eight years older than me. She: Thatcher admirer, now a far-right conservative politician. Home Secretary of the United Kingdom. Me: now here.

I was born on this earth and my parents' wish was that I would carry myself as a citizen as you do. From nation state to nation state I know that was never true, was always contingent. The partitioned ground of course will break beneath our feet

The first television news I remember as an awakening was of the British coal-miner's strike in 1984, when I was six years old. Patel would have been a young teenager then. It was described as the most *bitter and hard-fought* industrial action in British history, a rage against Thatcher, who brought rage back on the strikers. Her response hurt deeply in the Midlands, including around Cobridge, Stoke on Trent, where years later, a fourteen-year-old Muslim boy would disappear from school, a *terrorist* would grow up amidst severe economic disintegration.[100]

The conservative UK government, the billionaires, the architects of Brexit, might come from ancestral fortunes built on slavery or overseeing the establishment and maintenance of the civil service, the harvest of India; their chests swell as they now appoint the *native informant*,[101] turning shame   to pronounce *fear* of immigration; they see in   white nativism their own path to power. There is no 'moral rupture' here. No ambivalence between the legitimisation of the deed *and the morality by which we judge it*. They announce citizenship as a *privilege* and not a basic human right. For our own protection. As contingent citizens now wonder – from whom is permission to be or not to be sought? Who will grant the privilege of any body in this space and how should it show its *submission?* The answer comes in the Windrush scandal, the Grenfell fire, the generational damage caused by profiling; stop and search now embedded as code in the digital age. This is the story of punitive austerity, privatisation, expulsion, deportation of many   with a deep, long-lasting, a moral right to remain. The rise of the immigration detention centre, the closing of borders. The appropriation of language, emptying *revolutionary* words of meaning, tactics   as the use of decoys deploying personal stories, as Patel once did against opposition MP Florence Eshalomi to decry the Black Lives Matter movement and the systemic experience of race hate. All while standing inside the inner chamber of Parliament.[102]

While those who cast themselves (as the state story goes) out of citizenship and into prisons are even more reliant on the state's standards of human care: but this is a state without humanity, remember it is a term understood via its categories

We reach a place where we are who we say are, and what we seem to be, sometimes.

On the news in the days after the attack, I watched Patel walking with the Prime Minister, Boris Johnson, on London Bridge. Jack and I had taken a class in HMP Whitemoor just two days before. I had left incarcerated men there and was now holding   parts of their lives and past crimes, holding pages of their writing, sick with doubt I knew what was coming and at that moment could not speak. They would use the attack as reason to strengthen the punitive vengeance of the state on its citizens, particularly its racial and religious minorities, future residents of the prisons they planned to build, *as the carceral system will always use sensationalized cases and the spectre of unthinkable harm to create new mechanisms of disposability*[103]

We did not know then that in their hands, we were heading into the ravages the pandemic would wreak on a society stratified by race and class. I felt as a drowning   what I could not find the way to say publicly then: that they have no empathy: and this is a marker of having no shame. That their narrative of nation, of society's organisation, of home as castle and certain bodies and some peoples' position as ultimately inviolable, and of all of us, and *others* as completely contingent on that; makes them the most dangerous kind of human. And that lack risks all of us becoming more deeply incarcerated inside inhumanity each day.

The UK already has more prisoners per capita than any other country in western Europe. Almost a year to the day after the attack, it was announced that the number held in jails in England and Wales was just under 80,000, *and it would grow by 20,000 in the next five years, due to the recruitment of thousands more police officers, and tougher sentencing laws; £4 billion was being allocated to build 18,000 extra prison places.*[104]

I have been in the worst of places. Devoid of windows, though not devoid of care. To call it a *complex* is a metaphor. To call it a *disgrace* implicates us all in shame. I have faced this in the worst of ways – that the *monsters* that do the worst we can point to are the manifestations of our monstrous narratives, made from the city as we have constructed it. The lawmakers and ministers will redact their involvement, hide what they knew, accept no responsibility   they will never see prison; the rules we live by keep them safe. They police us, and fail us and still we trust them, as if we can abdicate for ourselves, and then hold them to account

CITIZENSHIP AND POLITICS:
A POSTCOLONIAL GLOSSARY

Citizens of the world (see: *citizens of nowhere* / *Commonweath citizens*) – The government of the atro-city has returned you to dust, now your names will be lost. You lived in the atro-city as

Funny tinge – As in, it is *not just about being black or a funny tinge … you know, different… B, err, from the BME community* – left wing politician Angela Smith used the words 'funny tinge' to describe British Asian (Bengali) journalist Ash Sarkar, the only person of colour on a live TV panel. Finally, you can stop calling yourself 'brown'.[105] You live in the aftermath of the

War on terror – Whose defining category is 'Muslim' whatever and however: in this context, the definition purposely seems to have no nuance and that is its great strength for the definer, not the defined   it is primarily for you that the

The Hostile Environment – Comes into existence: a web of legislation that turns us all into police, making it impossible for people of minority origin to feel free, in fact designed to make certain groups feel so unwelcome that they *choose* to exclude themselves. Everyday people check your right to study, right to rent, right to walk into a shop or airport or train station or through a university lodge with a backpack on. *The aim is to create, here in Britain, a really hostile environment for illegal immigrants.* And *others*   So Theresa May, then Home Secretary, later Prime Minister, said and did. In ideal terms for the fascist state, she wanted us to *choose* to go home – to permanently leave the UK, or *choose* not to try to come at all. There are deportation flights; and families being ripped apart. If people do live and stay, they are ferociously policed in the name of *keeping the public safe* by those who point away from themselves – there the *drug dealer*, there *stop and search*, there bad faith, there, there all of it shades of darkness, punishable with cultural silencing, a certain social narrative, police brutality and eventually prison and whatever they do inside. While outside the gates is a pernicious

Austerity – The end of shared social space: the defunding and closure of our libraries, our social centres, our play spaces, our community sports, an arid landscape in which the chance to create is hard won, made harder for

Citizens of nowhere / Commonwealth citizens – My grandmother's life forfeit in Partition, my mother in her womb. I know the state works to undermine communities' trust in each other and lead us in circles, to a condition of permanent fear and harm and from there to

Radicalisation – There are many theories about what *radicalises* a mind – The word itself is malleable, the word is a curve as horizon and used within poetry, theory, resistance, ideology as violence, for emancipation for causing terror (see also *terrorist*) after 9/11 while the new state seeks only to

Prevent – As if there is no cure for the *natural tendency* towards violent annihilation, they want you to fear, you now have a statutory duty to report the *Muslim* man next to you and report on children, report on neighbours, the hospital, the school, the university, HR department   must report on anyone *Muslim*, anyone who is pro-Palestine, who makes you *uncomfortable* (with apologies for the text as violence)   Prevent makes civil society into border police; all of us are meant to police in case of something.

There is much to understand about the danger / safety binary, the wide definitions of radicalisation and the climate of fear created and worked on within Prevent. The argument is that it turns young people from terrorism before they become radicalised. But it has proved damaging, sowing distrust, disillusionment and a dangerous isolation and affecting the opposite of what it says it wants to achieve. It has been discredited as Islamophobic, it has set up covert surveillance on young Muslims through youth radio projects, through art through other social networks. A British Muslim child, four years old, talking about the wildly popular computer game Fortnite has been referred. Another four-year-old says *cucumber*: nursery staff hear *cooker bomb*, and begin the process of referral. The Home Office says it has kept the public safe, but cases have been missed despite that; we have seen now that people can play the system to mask radicalisation while planning attacks.

In 2020, William Shawcross, a former director of a neoconservative think tank, and of the UK's Charity Commission was appointed by the government to lead the strategy. The papers write him so: under his tenure [the Charity Commission] was accused of institutional bias against Muslims, while Muslim groups highlighted comments he made in his book *Justice and the Enemy*, which appear to support the use of torture and the detention camp at Guantánamo Bay.

They quote him: *Europe and Islam is one of the greatest, most terrifying problems of our future. I think all European countries have vastly, very quickly growing Islamic populations.*

The climate of fear is in no way about to break. Its storm is let loose in the atro-city in the online words of powerful men the viral lode will take care of itself   as after *the event* the government applied the same flawed reasoning about how to identify a would-be *terrorist* to a *terrorist* at risk of recidivism, as if their scant knowledge would prevent   a bona fide[106]

Terrorist / terrorism – I know this word as certain men. I know this word is just a word. It has been understood by conservatives also as *non state political violence perpetrated naturally by people of colour on the left*   it has been reserved for Nelson Mandela and South Africa's ANC. For Palestinian resistance to Israeli occupation, the Irish right to self determination; Black liberation movements, animal rights movements   the word is wide, it will swallow Black Lives Matter protestors, *diaspora* Sikhs standing in solidarity with farmers in Punjab against the fascist Indian state; climate change activists; and *what should we call men who commit violence from a place of ideology?* – ★right wing fanatics, insurgents, extremists?

Lone wolves – See above★

Counter-terrorism – Will use the tools of surveillance, interrogation, incarceration, based on the underlying assumptions of what a *terrorist* looks like, in short they use *their* definition of the problem try to fix *the problem*   making fear a ley line, making trust a power game, so easy to play double-blind, hard to believe in

Desist and disengagement – Experience shows that many of those who are wedded to a political cause may never become totally disengaged but may still make the decision to desist,[107] they say, calling on

Culpability / credibility – The event happens. It is reported. It now has to become possible:

1. That trained criminologists and policing authorities can believe that a *terrorist* with a complex prison history and a firm grip on his narrative arc has the inner strength even to *desist* forget *disengage* from the persuasion of violence when he says and shows what they hear and see regardless of that history, the lure of the *Caliphate*

2. While authorities and senior editors at *The New York Times* will broadcast the voice and story of a Canadian man who says he was a *terrorist*; says he fought with ISIS in Syria, says he committed brutal violence and is now reformed and able to live a normal life among citizens in a flat above a shop. It is possible that those same experienced journalists and counter-terrorism experts will win awards for their podcast *Caliphate*, for their reportage. It is a fact that in December 2020, the paper will admit that this *terrorist* made his whole story up and was believed: the myth he made up was his own *radicalisation*

3. That when you find a book on countering *radicalisation* through partnerships between London Muslim communities and the London Metropolitan Police, by a man called Robert Lambert, published in 2011 you might find it useful. His authorial style is canonical. He writes about the draconion, top down policies of the state which ignore and worsen grass roots realities. He writes against hate preacher Anjem Choudhary, who, by then, has already converted the *terrorist* of this piece. He talks about anger, faith and political violence on Britain's

Islamophobic streets. Research makes you go further, and you find that for years he was a member of the Special Demonstration Squad, set up by police to gather undercover information on left-wing British protest groups. Stop the Vietnam war. Pro-Palestinian organisations. Anti-aparthied activists, the Campaign for Nuclear Disarmament (CND), Labour MPs. Which used the names and identities of 80 dead children as alias' for their operatives. Which for years operated covert surveillance on the family of Black teenager Stephen Lawrence, murdered in a racist attack in London in 1993, in an attempt to smear their campaign for justice and police accountability. Professor of Terrorism Studies, Robert Lambert, MBE (University of St Andrews, Scotland) was once undercover, to infiltrate an Animal Rights protest group. He had several relationships – one with a woman activist, and together they had a son. Then Lambert, or whatever name he went by, disappeared. Neither his partner nor son knew for decades that his identity was assumed, and he went free, which raises the question of[108]

Punishment – When should punishment begin? How intricate should it be? How far should it go before you cross your own border, *into the self you don't know yet you are?*[109] How young does that journey start, and when do you realise that you are locked within the

Prison industrial complex – We cannot address the myriad, interlocking injustices of a racist prison industrial complex without going to the roots of violence, which start with what we learn. By the start of the Fishmongers' Hall

Inquest – In which no one can say how it all went wrong, Witness A, MI5 will remain anonymous. The Home Secretary writes in support. *Seeking to justify redactions of other documents* on the grounds of public safety, human rights.[110] The undercover police want to remain anonymous for fear of terror reprisals. The press want the court to deny anonymity; to name (and shame) the former wife of the *terrorist*, though she hasn't seen her ex for years – they argue this is in the public interest – and that her fear of being doorstepped or attacked or her property graffiti'd never happens except in *fiction* as if this case was not more real than that seeking of

Equality – The desire to remain safe   I mean in   the dignity of a human life

In litany. In lament – As a question   that even in the face of traumatic violence   and our grief   when the linear text cannot but must always represent   continuity   can we imagine   a different world   with the language we have? I am sinking in

Water, as pani, as pain – I am meant to shape something out of tears. I cannot find a mould for them. All I have is

Language and trust – The beautiful, hopeful possibilities of those

where they meet a hybrid form. Hope to spend time with. The text is the carrier that is all this is for

Dignity –   None of us will survive this. Our only chance is to dismantle it. I want this as I want to love. Do not reconstruct it, do not reassemble it. Our only chance is to end it: I am talking about harm, the state's harm, the harm that punishes us before we are born: for the idea of us, our races and religions, for our class and genders, for our audacity in breathing hope as children. I am talking about the dignity of a life, of every life. I am talking about affinity as

Fiction as imagination – After backstory and event   there is a curve to consider. To be imagined is a kind of violence without the memory of true condition   of fiction as radical action. Which is not fiction, it is hope

ABOLITION

If we do not seek to hold all lives, to look, as Rich writes, steadily *at the thing itself,* we cannot mourn how they came to be, nor can we curtail the horror they will inflict. We begin to believe that we cannot change the world that makes people violent, that makes them kill: it will kill us.

This is a lament for all lives lost in a shameful system organised to harm, and in which a void is filled by violent ideology some choose to see through to death. This murderous system: that steals speech and legislates against positive action, meets terror as a solution, the only reliable continuity as narrative journey   in a broken life   fragmenting us from each other, and from hope.

Hope, which is a discipline, as Mariame Kaba reminds us.[111] To think about a world in which *others* will never make those same final choices makes me catch my breath

They say that abolition is a horizon, not an event. I see it behind me and in front as a curve

Ruth Wilson Gilmore, Angela Y. Davis, the abolitionist thinkers show us that though we struggle to imagine a world without prisons in all forms, we must try. In England, a *terrorist's* fatal actions make that revolution to hope so much harder for many. Real prison, real horror is the only solution, and the only place in our imaginations: a *terrorist* should be on indeterminate sentence, even *before* they can do actual harm.[112] Yes, it is fair, they say for the sake of public safety. I am ashamed to say that fairness is the balance of the sentence here. This is not a question of language but of life.

Let's consider instead the case of young Harry Vaughan, teenaged, not a *terrorist* but qualified as *neo-Nazi terrorist*, *far-right terrorist* as if the *terrorist* is not normally those things. And if splitting the argument over qualifying language seems unjustified here, let splitting be the active sensation — where justification is the concern — in a country where the fastest growing terrorist threat is from the far right,[113] young Harry — with straight As in his final school exams, with 14 terror charges, and two extra for possessing indecent images of children; had 4,200 images and 302 files in his devices, including an extreme right wing terrorist book, bomb making manuals, and a guide to killing people. He had documents about Satanism, Neo-Nazism and had downloaded and watched two child abuse videos, classified Category A — as prison: the most serious type. He lived at home with his parents, his father a clerk in the House of Lords. He was 'focused and able' so the judge said, and awarded him a two year suspended sentence – taking into account his diagnoses as on the autistic spectrum. His parents committed to helping him *change for the better.*[114]

This is not a call to expand the terminology of the *war on terror* in the name of anti-racism or a call for more, or longer, or more vicious incarceration. It is not a call to feed the prison's cells. Kundnani writes:

> *One key lesson to emerge from abolitionist thinking is that we should be wary of "reforms" that promise safety but actually add power and reach to law enforcement. To see the injustices in counter-terrorism law enforcement is to show how racialized fear works to validate amplified policing and incarceration more broadly.*

> *People are right to point out that there is a disparity in how white and Muslim perpetrators of mass violence are labelled. The way forward, though is not to broaden the use of the term 'terrorism' – and the assumptions and government practices that go with it – but to reassess the ways the country currently polices terrorism and probe more deeply into the social and political roots of racialised violence.*[115]

Atiya Husain agrees, saying that *terrorist* is not an inadvertently racist label that can be peeled off brown men and stuck onto white men. *Rather, the racial history and significance of the concept is constitutive of terrorism. The terrorist is a racial, epistemic, ideological and material other.*[116]

Would a different label have kept anyone alive? I think of Jack. And of Saskia, who I never got the chance to know. The violence perpetrated is narrativised *almost* as an inevitability, which makes it an easy thing to think about more punishment as the only recourse to *justice* we can imagine.

I am not making an argument for the release of extreme and high risk violent criminals in this moment now. I know danger is still present in prison and anywhere else. It is a reactive state. But in *We Do This 'Til We Free Us*, Kaba writes that questions like, *What about the really dangerous people?* are not questions a prison abolitionist must answer in order to insist the prison-industrial complex be undone.

The issue of danger, and of harm, and of the depravity and indignity of prison now, *the neglect, the denial of need; the fact they are places of suffering, violence, and death; they hurt and they injure and they destroy lives*[117] and their place in the atro-city are what we must face while we work for better at root. What can be changed *now* to build a more just world for many?

If the events of Fishmongers' Hall leave me any way out of loss, it is a recognition that the institutions of the atro-city, from which such violent harms arise, are *homegrown*, are no place of greater safety. We need new ways of holding ourselves as a society now, real transformations at the point of basic class, racial and gender justice. Restorative justice as a social transformation to heal community divisions caused by scarcities of so many kinds. Until perhaps forms of prison encoded in the curation of society, and prison itself are no longer considered a predicate for our 'civilisation' to continue.

The irony of calling on Neil Basu, Britain's most senior counter-terrorism police officer here is not lost on me, as in an interview he said:

> *Policies that go towards more social inclusion, more social mobility and more education are much more likely to drive down violence ... than all the policing and state security apparatus put together. It is much more likely to have a positive effect on society [....] The prescription for me is around social inclusion − it's social mobility, it's education, it's opportunity.*[118]

Now, in the aftermath, the UK government announces and passes the new Counter-Terrorism Bill, which will introduce mandatory minimum sentences of 14 years for the crime, as well as increasing powers of police and surveillance *broadening the definition of terror* − as

> *Funding for counter-terrorism policing will grow to £906 million in 2020 to 2021, a £90 million year-on-year increase. The money will support and maintain the record high number of ongoing counter-terrorism policing investigations and ensure a swift and effective response to terrorist incidents across the country, no matter where they take place.*[119]

Now the door is open: more and longer incarceration, what will happen inside to mitigate this against eventual release? Priti Patel has argued her support for the death penalty as a deterrent – now only doubled-back retribution on those the state wants to ring with *terrorist* can come.

What's required is a *jailbreak of the imagination*, as Kaba writes,[120] *in order to make the impossible possible*. To do this we might need fiction writers. But we might also need to address the conditions of the atro-city reading room. We might also return to think about violence as form and to consider the responsibility, if any, that mainstream literary culture has in the *trust and violence* loop.

Teju Cole takes the literary canon and offers it up as working example of the myth that fiction is a chance at empathy – that *reading* makes better humans of us – and argues that if this is true, then *Reader-in-chief*, President Barack Obama would have been less inclined to deploy drones. *Reader, he was not.* Cole rides the New York subway, a witness-survivor of 9/11: he has nowhere to go. Like Reemstma, like Butler, he takes *helpless refuge in literature again*, imagining *those in northwest Pakistan or just outside Sana'a* traumatised by drone strikes, *thinking I don't want to die.* He comes home to *rewrite the opening lines of seven well-known books*, from

> *Mrs Dalloway said she would buy the flowers herself. Pity. A signature strike leveled the florist's.*

to

Mother died today. The program saves American lives.[121]

But even Cole, one who has made it through the spiked gates of culture to the ground that whiteness claims as its right, must make terror feel safer for him by placing it in the hands of that distant Pakistani, that Yemeni, far across continents and oceans. Even as he writes, *there is a fear, too, a fear informed by the knowledge that whatever your worst nightmare is, there is someone out there embittered enough to carry it out.* He sends his gaze over the head of his neighbour's boy, his taxi driver's son, or those currently locked away. The bodies we carry and those we cannot speak of, the incarcerated in many forms

Ruth Wilson Gilmore writes, *Abolition is a totality and it is ontological. It is the context and content of struggle, the site where culture recouples with the political; but it's not struggle's form. To have form, we have to organise.*[122]

To ask what forms a *terrorist*,
or what form a *man* can take
in prison, to know the form of trauma in the aftermath
you can visit the curation of the reading room,
or you can read a novel and discuss it
in the lecture theatres of the atro-city
Either way if you want to *trust* the fiction writers
You better be ready to scream.

III.

RADICAL

HOPE

Cut them all, these wounded plants;
Don't leave them, whining, withered.
Pluck them all, these pained buds;
Don't leave them, writhing on the branch.

This crop of hopes, O friend,
Will, this time, too, be ruined.
All of days' and nights' labour
Will, again, bear no fruit.

In the field's crannies and cracks
Spread again the compost — your blood.

Again, water the soil – with your tears:
Again, plan for the next crop.

Plan for the next crop
When, again, we must suffer ruin.
If just one crop ripens, we shall have enough.
Till then, we must try again… and again…

'Yih faṣl umīdon kī hamdam'
('This Crop of Hopes, O Friends')
Faiz Ahmed Faiz, Montgomery Jail, March 1953[123]

And yet we are also somewhat reticent about any idea of right life in
literature. As the adage goes, wrong life cannot be lived rightly. And
the wrong life is the social whole. It is the life in which we participate
regardless of our intentions, the life of patriarchy, white supremacy,
and capitalist exploitation, to name only three aspects of wrong life.
The literary sits within this, as some old friends said, like a reading
room within a prison. It is fully enclosed. We would say there is no
right life within the literary, and that literary activism is the abolition
of the prison, not the better care of its reading room.

Wendy Trevino, Juliana Spahr, Tim Kreiner, Joshua Clover,
Chris Chen, Jasper Bernes[124]

THE SINGLE SHELF

There are two locked doors in the atro-city. One is real, one is fictional. One is in the citadel, high above ground; it opens into the reading room of the atro-city: somehow I have the key to it. Imagine this: in one corner, flames rise safely, merrily in the tiled, Victorian fireplace. There is a comfortable reading chair made of carved teak wood, a cushion hand-crewelled with leaves and vines and birds. On a low side-table, a pot of hot tea, a bone china cup, a bowl of sugar. Chocolate biscuits arranged on a plate. There is a single shelf, just out of reach, where a selection of fictions has accumulated. Heroes of the market, best-selling, critically acclaimed literary novels and short stories by writers whose names are known in reading rooms and classrooms and garlanded in awards from Cape Town to Juneau.

Many of us will only ever apprehend prison, or terror, or their related traumas through fiction: culture's power lies in its ability to shape the weather of the atro-city including through the stories on this shelf. They are magical, satirical, epic, hard-eyed and hybrid. They all deal in the seriousness of the harms we only want to encounter and understand through the safety of narrative imagination. Aleksandar Hemon reminds us that truth is an unstable category in fiction and nonfiction; and that *narration is the creation of truth, which is to say that truth does not precede it*[125]. Perhaps we can also say certain truths underpin narrative: the sense of an experience; the grounding in fact, the verisimilitude which forms the bedrock of a novel's world, the overall confidence the work puts forward – in the sense of sharing a secret it knows well. *How* it does so might underline a political sensibility as well as a writer's feeling for the world and its potential to be ordered.

A senior academic asked me recently in an interview what the word *literary* means to me: it means that which makes me literate in how to read the world, not only the one contained within a novel, but also the one which produces it. I welcome Alejandro Zambra's definition in *Not To Read*, translated by Megan McDowell of the kind of writer one might aspire to be, the books one might want to read:

> *Books say no to literature. Some. Others, the majority, say yes. They obey the market or the holy spirit of governments. Or the placid idea of a generation. Or the even more placid idea of a tradition. I prefer books that say no. Sometimes, even, I prefer the books that don't know what they are saying.*[126]

Saying *yes* to this, I also know well that no single shelf of the literary is conceivable in the Western imagination without Shakespeare. The question of what makes us human is as constant as the asking of what makes Shakespeare perennial. The citadel is produced by the culture that it protects, after all. Now, in the atro-city, inside the reading room, fiction is all I have left. Margaret Atwood's *Hag-Seed*, a retelling of Shakespeare's *The Tempest* set in a contemporary Canadian *correctional institute* is the first book that falls from the shelf.

Hag-Seed's title is culled from one of the names given to Caliban, the creature shackled and abused as *abhorr'ed slave* by the charismatic Prospero, exiled Duke of Milan who has taken over power on Caliban's island home. On the UK hardback: a black cover, a red eye, a series of white lines suggest a storm, suggest sleeplessness; the effect is reminiscent of enraged ape-eyes. Here is Caliban the prisoner, the animal. In the early 19th century, William Hazlitt argued that *The Tempest*'s protagonist was *not Prospero but Caliban, the play's true victim of exile and dispossession*.[127] Since then the play has been read as a nautical chart of the early modern transatlantic world; the enslavement and transportation of African lives to service Britain and America; as the antecedent of the British Empire, against the enslavement of millions by whiteness and its language, English, and as contemporary critique of racial injustice. Prospero is understood as coloniser, chief punisher, torturer. Caliban the motherless, the fatherless, the subservient (un)natural poet, dreaming freedom, practicing violence, created by the conditions of his enslavement.

But *Hag-Seed*'s focus is not Caliban's freedom, or the terrors of the world that made him. Instead Atwood centres Prospero, here imagined as lovable but deluded Felix, Artistic Director for the local theatre festival. Felix is imprisoned in grief: his wife, and then his three-year-old daughter Miranda, who is named for Prospero's daughter in Shakespeare's play have died. When he is usurped from the festival by his nemesis Tony he exiles himself to a bunker in the woods, nursing his dreams of revenge. Years pass, and he takes a job as a 'teacher of Literacy through Literature,' at Fletcher Correctional Institute. The programme is meant to train incarcerated men to high-school standards (most of them stalled at third grade, we are told) so they can one day become productive members of society.

Eschewing the usual set-text, Felix insists on teaching Shakespeare: he gets astonishingly good results. When Tony, now a government Minister, schedules a visit to Fletcher to see the programme for himself, Felix decides to get his revenge and expose Tony's corruption while fulfilling his lifelong dream of staging *The Tempest*, starring himself as Prospero. It will be done in the prison, during the visit. The men will take supporting roles.

Hag-Seed's tone of magical, delighted farce is dismissive of the anti-racist lens through which *The Tempest* has long been examined. Instead, as Felix constantly reminds his students (and Atwood reminds her readers), *Shakespeare can be read in numerous ways*. Through Felix, who, differently from, say, David Lurie in JM Coetzee's *Disgrace* is written uncritically despite the tone of farce in the novel, Atwood seems to want to rehabilitate *The Tempest* from established race-criticism while reinscribing colonial violence. The resulting white saviour narrative can only be read as a move to save Atwood's white Shakespeare as culture itself.[128]

Following Macaulay's 1835 dictum that *a single shelf of a good European library was worth the whole native literature of India and Arabia*,[129] as Atwood writes, *The Fletcher Correctional Players only do Shakespeare because that is the best and most complete way of learning theatre*; let us read *learning theatre* as *becoming civilised* here, following the correlation of world and stage that Shakespeare insists on. Meanwhile, Felix is the kind of director who appropriates inequality for titillation on stage. His early ambition for his *Tempest* sees him dreaming that his *Caliban would be a scabby street person – black or maybe Native – and a paraplegic as well, pushing himself around the stage on an oversized skateboard*. Twelve years later, now teaching in prison, he finds fifteen incarcerated men who want to play the monster. Finally the role goes to Leggs: *Mixed background, Irish and black*, as Felix notes, though in a kind of classic Atwoodian double-backing, his blackness is erased into *Red hair, freckles, heavy build, works out a lot*. As Daniel Swift points out, Leggs never reaches the heights of Caliban's poetic voice.[130] His awful half-rap, ventriloquised by Atwood, instead has him accepting his animal status: *My name's Caliban, got scales and long nails, / I smell like a fish and not like a man … I'm Hag-Seed*.

Embodying Caliban's most famous lament, *You taught me language, and my profit on 't / Is I know how to curse!*[131] Felix uses Shakespeare's language as his tool to manage his students' obedience in class: he limits their profanities to curses from the set play. Of the (hundreds of) extremely interesting curses she might have quoted from 37 plays, Atwood chooses a racially inflected one to demonstrate Felix's method: *You could only say, 'The devil damn thee black, thou cream faced-loon' if the play is Macbeth.* And when the men list *earth* as a swear word from *The Tempest* because, one man says, of *colonialism*, Felix thinks sarcastically to himself: *Multiculturalism at its finest.* He tells the class, *earth* is merely *the opposite of air here. It's supposed to mean low down*, ignoring the obvious association of brown dirt and the questions of land, of dark men's bodies and domination over both that so trouble *The Tempest* and its interlocutors. Yet in his notes, Felix writes that Caliban should be *earthy, potentially violent.* The appeal to the racist trope hardly needs spelling out.

Hag-Seed is populated by ghosts, doublings and illusions: some made digitally, others conjured by grief, paranoia or mistrust. But overwhelmingly what haunts this novel is the white fear of racialised bodies as inherently violent and untrustworthy, as uncivilised; the assertion upon which white supremacy stakes its cultural claims. In the world of the novel outside the prison, these bodies are kept safely in constant service: Tony walks around with security guards who are described only as being one *black* and one *brown*; Thai nail bars are noted on the town's poorer fringes: all based in fact, one might say and deployed to underpin the fictions of the rest.

Inside Fletcher Correctional, this anxiety is mediated by Atwood's reassurance that that the men are non-violent offenders, held in medium security: their crimes are semi-amateur drug dealing, theft from banks, breaking and entering cars and convenience stores. One is a genius hacker (who gets the role of Ariel), another a con man and identity theft specialist. There's a renegade doctor and an accountant from a respectable firm. A lawyer and Ponzi scheme scammer. All except Leggs / Caliban – the junkie, war veteran, in prison for violent assault. (There is a passing reference to the men in the high-security wing who Felix never sees or hears from: they are locked safely out of the novel.)

Felix's relationship to the men is half fatherly pride as he watches their self-esteem grow through the Shakespeare he teaches them; half fearful, as he remains convinced that he is at risk of being harmed by them, that the acting skills he is teaching them will be misused for crime. But when they speak Shakespeare's language they are redeemed.

Civilising the natives through the teaching of English literature was Macualay's project: it rests on the denigration of the *other* – as in contemporary London and in the UK, Black youth culture's *homegrown* sound, drill music is routinely blamed by police for fuelling violence. It is used in court as evidence of actual intent or confession and associated in the justice system with encouraging criminal behaviour. Earlier bans, Criminal

Behavior Orders and gang injunctions against drill artists have been imposed, blurring the lines between art and artist in dangerous ways that enable the carceral state to 'work'. Setting up Shakespeare as Atwood does via *The Tempest* in a prison could have been an opportunity to write a more equal music and not for more fraught drawing of lines. Real world examples such as the work of Akala[132] exist if one wishes to be inspired by them.

One might argue that the men in Felix's class are diverse. *They range in age from nineteen to forty-five. They are many hues, from white to black through yellow, red and brown; they are many ethnicities.* Let us instead call this, after Danita J. Dodson, the *paradigm of denial*,[133] where in real terms, Indigenous[134] and Black[135] men are disproportionately incarcerated in Canada. Atwood instead seems to be aiming for what Bruce Miller, the director of the television adaptation of Atwood's most famous work, *The Handmaid's Tale,* described as 'post-racial'. But *The Handmaid's Tale* (as novel and series) has been widely criticized for its theft of the histories of oppression of Black and brown women and the erasure of our voices and our ancestors' experiences in their world-making.[136] Priya Nair points out that *understanding [The Handmaid's Tale] requires looking beyond the obvious and into what is absent,*'[137] and the same can be said for *Hag-Seed,* in which the men are merely waiting for Prospero to teach them, even to tame them with Shakespeare, as with the anger-management therapy Felix says some have had.

The quality of Atwood's mercy does strain through *Hag-Seed*: there are glancing references to prisoner suicide rates, depression, and the fragile egos that relish applause even as they support one anothers' efforts with rare camaraderie. Despite Felix's biases, he has a pedagogy taken straight from many who teach in prison – he insists that as far as possible, the problems of prison life are left at the classroom door; each person, no matter what their educational attainment level gets a clean slate coming in and is supported to think of themselves as actor / writer / technician / set designer / whatever the workshop is offering for that hour of respite. Atwood is also particularly astute on the ways in which individuals and institutions, from academia to government, profit from 'rehabilitative' education programmes. Overall, the constant sense one gets from the novel is that such programmes are a good thing (especially to those delivering them), meanwhile prison can be made nicer (especially through Shakespeare). But incarceration is ultimately necessarily (on the epic level of Shakespeare) to keep society safe – particularly from racialised men.

Felix's own sense of safety is contingent on his troupe remaining incarcerated, and also shackled to him as their teacher. When a group of the men say they have imagined an afterlife for Caliban, Felix thinks, *Caliban has escaped the play. He's escaped from Prospero, like a shadow detaching itself from its body and skulking off on its own.* He cannot imagine the monster could walk straight, head high into a world shared with his former master. The prisoners then speculate that Caliban *might go after everyone who used to treat him in a bad way. Do a whole revenge thing [...] pick them off one by one –*

And Prospero? And Miranda? Felix asks.

The men respond, *Maybe Caliban forgives them, maybe he doesn't. Maybe he stalks them, jumps them, goes to work with his claws. We're still working on* – becoming human, and able to breathe. Then the Hag-seeds ask Felix *shyly* to direct their sequel one day, in another world where they are all *free*, he nods even as he thinks, *Now there's no one to restrain him. Will Prospero be spared, or will retribution climb in through his window one dark night and cut his weasand? Gingerly, he feels his neck.* But why should he feel that their freedom would put him in danger?

The novel ends with Felix about to embark on a holiday cruise. He decides to take 8Handz, *genius black-hat hacker* who played Ariel and who has been *granted early parole,* with him. Felix will give some lectures, and imagines 8Handz at his side, earning his keep by performing Shakespeare monologues on the voyage for a fee.

I imagine this *freed man*, this contemporary minstrel, a travelling player in a bond of gratitude; I have to stop. Swift notes that *complaining that Margaret Atwood is insufficiently attuned to the politics of storytelling is as absurd as accusing Shakespeare of the same failing.*[138] Before the conclusion, the chain of connection is painful enough.

Before beginning work on *The Tempest*, Felix asks the men to count the prisons in Shakespeare's play. There are nine, he says – including the play itself. But *Hag-Seed* gives us ten. Felix is the prison of whiteness embodied and externalised; his eye as it sees is nothing but the illusion of his powerful self. Of all the prisoners in this story, only the restless ghost of his daughter, pale Miranda, dead twelve years, is finally allowed to go free. bell hooks writes, *there is a gap between the values they claim to hold and their willingness to do the work of connecting thought and action, theory and practice to realize these values and thus create a more just society.*[139] To set *The Tempest* in a prison in contemporary times and not have it be about racial justice in some profound ways – instead to offer it as a kind of antidote of rehabilitative whiteness to that interpretation – is as disappointing (if unsurprising) as the book being commissioned and published in the Hogarth Series of Shakespeare re-tellings, named for the Bloomsbury group, neither of which include writers of colour, though in their work dark bodies are often imagined, and written onto and about.

I close the book gently, thinking about Felix and what teachers in prison do when they come and they go. While it is possible to ask people to leave prison life outside the room, and to construct a course where that might happen, it should not be the case that the person teaching it does not know their histories, and their life contexts inside. How can they keep everyone safe, when art, as a practice, is also a portal? Am I demanding too much from fiction? Now, alone among *The Tempest* and the wreck, I note Mikhail Bakhtin's words:

> *We are constantly and intently on the watch for reflections of our own life on the plane of other people's consciousness, and moreover,*

not just reflections of particular moments of our life, but even reflections of the whole of it. And while seeking to catch these reflections, we also take into account that perfectly distinctive value-coefficient which is completely different from the coeffecient with which we experience our own life in ourselves.[140]

Reading fiction can be like that. Can welcome us home or shut us down. Setting the tone for an inclusive imaginative space rests with the most powerful writers. Is that something to ask? Or is it time to simply walk away?

Now to the other locked door. I have not been able to return there since November 28, 2019. To enter as a vistor, you must be police-checked, security-registered, and accompanied by at least one carrier of keys. You will be advised not to wear ripped jeans or tight or short clothes: you will leave your phone. You will pass through airport style security, a body search. Go down corridors, across the cold yard. Up and then down stairwells and wait on either side of double-locked, barred gates, as the sounds and size of them moving forces you to think of them never opening; as the progress you make through this maze, which is designed to strip you of your autonomy by degrees, works on you; you know that you have no choice in this, you acquiesce to it as a person moves to board a plane someone else will fly. Down again, down again, to where two security guards, both white, flank the door. They gesture to you to come through. Inside, the writers are working on their craft.

THE POINT OF DEPARTURE

There is an everyday feeling to this building. An everyday car park, standard issue signage, mass-produced red brick walls. It could be a hospital, a new university building – a school perhaps. The college students, all born in the decade around 9/11 or 7/7 are used to surveillance and reception desks behind reinforced glass and to taking off shoes and coats and belts and the rest of it. After the first visit or two, even the fingerprint check and the armed security feel *almost* normal.

The point of departure – the moment that high-security prison becomes reality for these students comes to each in turn. It might happen when she has to make that joke *again* about the one whose fingerprint, week after week, can't ever be read by the device; ha ha, *she'd make the perfect criminal.* It might be crossing the yard between security gates, like that walk from a terminal building to the waiting plane, when you place part of your trust in experts who you will never meet – it might come as they all taste the metallic cold in the air – and behind the high, barbed wire fence can see the sterile area. It is not much more landscaped than the gravel across which she and the group of young people are walking. The group itself has to be constantly reminded to stay together, to keep in a tidy line – they have not yet properly registered where they are; they haven't all reached the point yet – though she can see on some of their faces, the quieter ones, walking quickly, silently – they have.

Perhaps it comes for the rest of them as they walk through the corridors, stop for those double locked gates to be opened for them, shut behind them; the light becoming less; the windows becoming smaller, suddenly disappearing; though they walk the same route each time there are moments of disorientation, the giving over of autonomy to the trust that someone else will keep you safe – she has felt the same happen in hospitals. She thinks that for most of them it comes after they turn through a small side door and go down metal staircases, past yellow painted walls hung with large canvases. No one asks who the artists are, where they are now. Through the final door, this could be a basement, could be the ground floor, there's no way to tell. A nod to the guards, and they are into the workshop, now the teaching room: the familiar hot water caddy, plastic cups, a roll of digestives; the plastic trestle tables, the flip chart, name stickers (first names only) and biros: they enter the room with a sense of release; forgetting for a moment that they cannot leave till the end.

When the men arrived, one by one, they were searched and then unlocked to join them; there was always a shift to swagger in the room like a plane taking off, turbulence through clouds and then the sudden levelling – the sight of familiar faces, the settling in, catching up and beginning to *free write* – cruising altitude reached.

In the first two years, the teaching room was actually the hall used as the prison mosque; it was empty but for a set of hard chairs around those plastic trestle tables, and the prison guards had a lectern though this was not always the case. In this room she was the teacher. This was now the place where student writers worked.

Each one came in and made an effort to leave *heavy* outside the door. Prison as violence, as paranoia, as stories within stories, as attack and defence. As madness   instead each one came as the person they wanted to be. Everyone was nervous, at first. Everyone fronting a little bit. It could have been any writer's room, except for the mix of writers in the room, and except for the prison guards.

It was a program bringing together young people with men inside a high-security prison. The stakes – emotional, educational – were so high. It was obvious that that there was an agreement between the men – and a striving between the *guests* – the effort was tangible – not to make any assumptions about anyone in the best way. It was not a question of naïvety or suspicion. It was just that a group of people had come together to practice a few hours of creativity against the highest set of odds an advanced late-capitalist society can make, within its own borders. Yes, I'll say it. There was hope.

The time was outside time. No matter who they were and what they did outside this room, stories would leak out of their ears and eyes and hands onto the page. The usual clanging sounds of prison muted now for class. And as for the writer who was also the teacher, who knows what anyone was expecting?

She told them she was there as a teacher, not a snitch (unless she had to be for safety's sake, which was implied), and definitely not as a writer to cull stories of life inside from them. Why was she really there? To work. To show how writing, as work, could be a source of encouragement, of courage, or could help in building self-esteem. The deeper answer was obscure to her, just as it is to many thousands of people who teach arts in prisons – she had the chance to be there and took it as a question of how to be in the world, and this is the only form I can use to write about it now. She's safe there – in the third person – I can't violate the trust between me and her, the way she *remembers* that time. Whoever was in the room was there: she repeatedly asked for and was not given *the whole story*   at the time, it was all about trust.

The point of departure wasn't actually the realisation *this is a high-security prison, there is danger in creative writing here*. It was in the acceptance of that. Call it *risk management*. It was in the way that the hours passed quickly. There was often the generous laughter of an unlikely collection of people coming together to lay down some insecurities through focus on craft, and the way people were considerate with each other's work. Then the time ended with a body search of half the group, while the other half pretended not to notice. In the way some being searched bantered with the officers, and others silently endured it. The way others lingered, trying to avoid it. It was in the way some of the students were able after those classes to write letters to their children more openly than they had before. The way the university students mostly all fell asleep in the minibus on the drive back. Across the flat lands to the quiet, worn, ivy-covered stones of their Cambridge college, arriving at evensong. It happened like that each time.

She would walk home across the green and through the November dark, using her phone as a torch, only able to see the single next step. Prison has an indescribable smell that permeates clothes; just as a sense of hope in forging some connection in a classroom lingers in the mind. The small moments: everyone liked a phrase someone wrote, someone who rarely spoke in class called out the set-poem for its misrepresentation of a local place he once knew. Or seeing the young students stop thinking for at least half an hour about how at university they never felt white enough, man enough, good enough, smart enough, cool enough, thin enough, because no one in that room was interested in those things: they were just all so present.

She knew the course could not address, reverse or eradicate the wider harms that had happened, or were waiting. The prison considered the activity low risk because it was education, and it happened in a low risk area of the prison. They were not thinking about the risk assessment of *creative writing*   and the meeting of   vulnerabilities   few *organisationally*   seemed to take that seriously. Looking for mirrors of *hope*

Later, the lawyers would ask her if she remembered him. If he stood out

She remembers them all, their faces, their names, the trauma and the risk of their work, the danger of all that was submerged always alive in the room. She had no safety except to use *craft* to protect them from   all of them.

There was everything that no one would ever know about each of them, except the stories they chose to tell, and in the silences, and in reading between the lines. There was a kind of trust in that room: perhaps enough to form the basis of a moral life. In those hours, it had to be enough.

To survive in a prison, to teach in that way, you have to trust you won't go mad.

A confrontation with the self, as if tasting mortality, sometimes happens when a plane leaves the ground. It may not be conscious, but you can sense it in your mouth and the popping of your ears as you are carried through clouds. Like the intimate realisation, not often confronted, that some university students have as they come into prison. When finally, the brutal logic of the atro-city, which they are considered the elite citizens of, and which keeps their university largely pristine while so many people of colour are incarcerated, is revealed by simple dint of numbers. This perhaps is proof of the doubt they taste when they arrive at Cambridge, so many of them think of themselves as not worthy: that their admission must be some mistake. It is not, of course: they have been lucky *and* worked hard *and* been selected for many reasons – yes of course sometimes including their names. But now they know what they have never been told and never will be until they choose to put themselves forward for work like this: their instinct was also right. In simple terms, they cannot unsee. The numbers prove the myth inscribed in our education system by denial of its carefully managed segregationist practices: white students are intelligent, and deserving. Black and Asian / Muslim students are not. Here is the confrontation with the theory of race as biology decided by white *explorers* centuries ago.

Some of them feel shame, some relief. Some pray alone, and continue writing together. There is an alchemy, there is a sense of striving that is completely real. Whatever happens in the encounter, it translates. Decisions must be made.

In those sessions, she asked them all not to talk about the stories they would share with each other, or discuss each other's writing outside the room, unless it was a question of safety. Breaking this trust here, I tell myself that she did not know then that there would be an aftermath, there would be the shadows of ten deep prisons to contend with, there would be fear of taboos, there would be conviction; there would be the memory of laughter and shared stories   and of knives. There would be no more sleep.

THE PROPHET

A paradise cannot be lost. Fiction writers are not prophets. They are at best weather people. But sometimes the two get confused in culture, and after 9/11 when ash fell on New York like snow in September, the writer Don DeLillo walked to Ground Zero with his editor.[141] He wrote a piece which was published in the *Guardian* in December 2001. It was classified under FICTION, making him, I think, the first novelist to use the form to write about that event for a global Anglophone audience.

'In The Ruins of The Future' is in many ways predictive, calling into being the shattered world from which I write this now. What does that make DeLillo and his art? *A New Yorker* piece published in 2011 by Martin Amis sets up the provocation that DeLillo wants to make; it is titled 'Laureate of Terror, Don DeLillo's Prophetic Soul.'[142]

Prophet. Stare at this word. Experience it in phonetic syllables. Pro-fet. Wonder at its mystery. Think of its origins.

Its many meanings. Its relationship to *terror* as we have been forced by culture to interpret the word embodied since 9/11. Its function here seems almost casual; DeLillo has been writing fiction about terrorism since 1977. And yet there is nothing casual about the inference that somehow this fiction writer can claim a title millions of Muslims consider holy; the language is the subtle battle ground   or maybe just *a wink*

'In The Ruins' is a treatise on what makes an Islamist *terrorist* different from a Christian one (or a white Christian one). It ends with the narrator walking the grieving avenues of New York and passing a woman praying to Mecca on a street corner in full sight of many, using the Manhattan grid to orientate herself. 'Allahu akbar', DeLillo writes for her. (And for *readers*, who it was assumed in 2001, needed it, the piece translates this as, *God is great*.)

Amis says, *Very broadly, we read fiction to have a good time – though this is not to deny that the gods have equipped DeLillo with the antennae of a visionary. There is right field, and there is left field. He comes from third field—aslant, athwart.* I remember the feeling of falling down the chute of DeLillo's slanted thinking when I first read the story. Thinking about what it means to me to read and if it was ever to *have a good time*. I remember the disorientation I felt in its insistent binaries of us vs. them; of Christianity vs. Islam endorsed in a liberal newspaper; the depiction of an understandable, forgivable white terror against the inexplicable monster, the Islamist. Reading the story again now, twenty years later, I recognise the deep shock and rupture it sought to capture and contain, even as I still feel its harm. Revisiting it, I am back to the sense of chaos he evoked   the immediate aftermath

Years have gone by and in the rubble of this moment, I feel as if I am standing on a precipice, surveying what is left, seeing a ladder of sentences fall away beneath me, made of the rungs of the world DeLillo wrote into being when I was fresh out of college.

I remember reading and trying to write DeLillo's sentence making, his sense making, his making sense of:

1. Capital markets. He wrote: *The internet summoned us all to live permanently in the future… there is no memory there* (and thinking I would remember this story)

2. Narrative: *Today the world narrative belongs to terrorists* but not the ones fighting global capitalism in Seattle. DeLillo meant the *other* ones, 9/11 bombers. It was America that *drew their fury – the blunt force of our foreign policy* […] *It was the power of American culture to penetrate every home, wall, life and mind.*

3. Motive: *The terrorists of September 11*, he wrote, *want to bring back the past.*

4. Plots: the sentence that stayed with me most strongly was this: *We are rich, privileged and strong, but they are willing to die.* Also, *Plots* (theirs) *reduce the world.*

5. Qualification: The story asserts such a *terrorist* is: *not the self-watcher, the soft white dangling boy who shoots someone to keep from disappearing into himself.* (See previous ★lone wolf)

6. Conclusion: that the American *justice system's provision for the rights of the accused can only seem an offence to men bent on suicidal terror.*

I wonder today if this is DeLillo playing misdirection, appealing to us to think about bias by presenting the founding myths that form whiteness as fact. Listing them in the story as ironic appeal to our better sensibilities, our sense of history. But the whispering part of me also reflects upon what Toni Morrison and others might say about the American justice system. About the rights of 'the accused' in America. What about that.

In the rubble of the atro-city, in the ruins of a future, all I have left is something I began with, and when I come to it, find DeLillo has already said.

The event itself has no purchase on the mercies of analogy or simile. We have to take the shock and horror as it is. But living language is not diminished. The writer wants to understand what this day has done to us. Is it too soon?[…] In desertion of every basis for comparison, the event asserts its singularity. There is something empty in the sky. The writer tries to give memory, tenderness and meaning to all that howling space.

Years have gone by. I am trying to find a way from singularity. At London Bridge, November 2018, *Operation Plato* was launched: *a set of tactics or strategies for responding to a marauding terrorist attack.* In *Tragedy Since 9/11*, the last book I buy before I leave Cambridge, Jennifer Wallace writes: *The repetition is an indication of a lack of resolution, the lack of a conclusion. Our lament for* [those who died in the twin towers], *for New York and for whatever 9/11 represents, is without closure, stuck fast in the state of melancholic trauma. All that can be done is to metaphorically wail the lament, the aie/aiai of tragedy,*[143] in the Western sense

Years have gone by. I am *the writer* who was inside the prison. No prophet-laureate-visionary the type   more likely to be lost. Is all I can do lament? Here instead is my reckoning. As an attempt to say the reverse of what has already been said by DeLillo before he wrote 'In the Ruins of the Future':

> *There's a curious knot that binds novelists and terrorists… Years ago, I thought it was possible for a novelist to alter the inner life of a culture. Now bomb makers and terrorists have taken that territory. They make raids on human consciousness. What writers used to do before we were all incorporated.*[144]

I am making a new ladder to climb out of the rubble, and it is still in formation

1. I reject the *alteration* from either side: the devil or the divine

2. Culture is as culture does and that is manifest and I think DeLillo wrote that somewhere, too

3. I reject incorporation, the manners of cultural capital that decides for millions *what to read*

4. DeLillo publishes his story, and then asks *is it too soon?*[145] The answer exists in the aftermath, the writing that follows the event.

I am in fragments, walking north, and maybe holding what remains. In the rubble, what lives come next

FALLING PREY

After Fishmongers' Hall, there were further *terrorist* attacks by men who had been incarcerated, and one by perpetrators who were still inside Whitemoor. The victims were prison staff. The question of *radicalisation* in UK prisons, consistently pressing, came to the fore in the media again.

Yes, she acknowledged this word *radicalisation* as one of the ghosts in the writing room. She greeted it each time, even as she greeted the spectre of sexual violence or murder or theft, or any of the histories that she had to learn for herself that the men carried. She needed to know. In order, as much as any writing teacher can, to keep the students safe as they shared stories   beginners at fiction often write   a stone's throw from their lives. She Googled, and had to sit with that, and what she found.

The idea that such men should get to take a writing class is a difficult one for some to stomach. There are victims who cannot speak, will never speak again.

She goes into prison sensing that perhaps there are people in charge who want to believe in *rehabilitation* as a mask for *redemption*. There's a form of white saviourism at work here, which is more about the redeemer than the *other*. It's an institutional violence, when the *program* is considered more important overall than the people within it. A sense of that lingers as teaching continues. She does not know / it is not widely disclosed that   their *values*, their *policy* rests on *theodicy*; like June Jordan, she would consider this approach a *fundamental flaw*. Faith can enhance a form of politics in prison. While forms of it are also a solace, or can seem hollow in a life sentence. Growth on a path comes out of trauma. Personal development, or the ability to concentrate, to finish something, and redraft it, to share it and get feedback – is one thing – perhaps restorative, for a time. It is possible to present a calm demeanour and take feedback and be polite just to get into the room, and stay in it, and enjoy the escape of creativity as a means to survive the day. To let that feed a different kind of special narrative is something she avoids. Never praises the result, only the effort of making. And it is not growth as evidence of constant good as a journey to a better humanity, even if it points to hope. Neither can it work in a vacuum. At least she goes into the workshop knowing that.

She thinks it is dangerous to offer the world a story of salvation: of relentless resilience, or of linear progress. To commodify into performance vulnerability or 'success.' Or even to insist on LOVE without any acknowledgement that harm affects people in profoundly different ways that must be fully understood. Otherwise isn't this work just a part of *the formal network of the lie?*

Solitary becomes a way of thinking about oneself in any world; a form of basic survival is predicated on what has been destroyed. Some say – *the damage is permanent, no matter how well camouflaged,*[146] and she can't help but wonder – is that all life is? The ability to believe and to present one's own camouflage convincingly enough to pass through pain to something else – the opposite of hope or hope itself? And what exactly, when someone is so very damaged, and so high-risk, so dangerous, when lives are lost can we hope for?

The question of radicalisation in society, or in prison, then shares markers with other kinds of misdirected need for safety, status, brotherhood. Perhaps it also rests in the power that continuity, however twisted, offers to a shattered mind or broken life, even to those that appear to be whole. If its tactics are bullying, persuasion, or a push and pull between acceptance and exile from the group, then a closed prison is a perfect place for it to multiply. Safety in this context is a myth. Meanwhile, the solace of faith is a cornerstone of millions of lives. Of course not all converts will become radicalised, or extreme, or violent. But in some extreme cases that path might be the only authority that promises something that can be self-delivered and achieved in a lifetime of precarity. In that sense it will never let you down.

In every classroom, cliques and gangs and exchanges of power, attachments form and fluctuate; a question of safety, of dignity and reputation operate along the frequencies the atrocity sets. There is risk. Bolted on to an absolute conviction that something more is to come. What is different about prison as she experienced it is not too much, except the level at which emotions, and their suppression; at which oppression and violence and need for recognition come out in the performance, in class. The prison writer's room is one example of vulnerability – which exists in any writer's room – but in prison it is heightened, for everyone. And always surrounded by what lies outside.

If in our lives we seek out community that makes us feel good: filling a void – why wouldn't it be the case that in the interminable pressure of a long sentence, you might not do the same, whether you really believed in a God, or political or social damage, or personal victimhood, or your own potential – which needed constant validation that you were special – whether that belief, the way it is spoken to you is all you have to moderate your time? You might struggle, you might succumb. You might write a song, a poem, a play. You might write

YOU AS THE TERRORIST: YOU IN THE ROOM

Following 9/11 Judith Butler writes that we use the narrative *I* after violent, traumatic events, to make up for the decentring wound *we* have suffered (the italics are mine – an implicit question as to whom *we* include). Drawing on Black feminist abolitionist thinking, Butler's is a call to write away from this patriarchal form, this authority – to think about the queerness and solidarity of grief in community. Trauma cannot be written, or survived, in the first person singular.

In fiction or writing about terror, the 'second person' becomes a formal response; voicing trauma as a way of building empathy. For some writers of South Asian-origin it seems to bring the sense of *the other* closer than the first person; it offers a complicated ambivalence and the familiar experience of self as ambiguous. It allows an address, and imagines the reader alive and present in the text; or is even the text being read. There is the question of splitting, and of understanding. There is the implication of collusion. There is danger in it. There is the point that if a brown man is only fully developed in fiction writer's country, you cannot write yourself out of it. There's Levinasian ethics to it, for those interested in thought underpinnings.[147]

Butler says, *the ability to narrate ourselves not from the first person alone, but [to] receive an account delivered in the second can actually work to expand our understanding of the forms that global power has taken*.[148]

As a way of thinking about the *terrorist*, or those Others trapped in the spirals of 'far-off' wars, the second person address is embraced by Western-orientated terror-lit culture. Mohsin Hamid's Booker-shortlisted *The Reluctant Fundamentalist* is one such example, called (unlike so many *cacophonous*, *lush*, *vibrant* postcolonial novels), *admirably spare and amazingly exciting*.[149] Hamid's Paskistani hero situates you within his story of landing at Yale, and then, to his delight at a prestigious, high paying job as a management consultant as 9/11 takes place. In the aftermath he experiences the humiliation of airport stop and search and constant profiling, making the racist microagressions he is frequently subject to no longer tolerable. Eventually he leaves America and returns to a Pakistan already terrorised by American drones and more.

In the novel, his direct address to *you* establishes paranoia, and plays on preconceptions of who the reader is trained to trust. White elites of New York? Brown elites of Pakistan? The educated, the civilised? Do we mean lovers of Shakespeare and opera or of ghazals and qawwalis? Or the unheimlich hybrid *both*? Hamid shows us how violence transmutes through American culture, policing and profiling, and suggests how it might finally be met in American blood. However this is only a suggestion: the writer never concludes that the charming narrator is part of a *terrorist* cell. The reader is left to question either his own perception of narrative truth or his anti-Muslim bias.[150]

Hamid's novel and his choice of form has a literary predecessor in 'Weddings and Beheadings,' a short story by Hanif Kureishi which was nominated for the UK's National Short Story Prize in 2006,[151] just three years after the US-led invasion of Iraq, and the same year Iraq's deposed dictator, Saddam Hussein, was hanged. Al Qaeda was in ascendance by then, and Kureishi's narrator is a young Iraqi filmmaker who survives by filming both Iraqi weddings *and* beheadings for the terrorist group. He addresses the reader directly – here 'you' is used to frame a war, frame the reader, frame the brutality of being coerced into collusion with violence. *You don't know me personally. My existence has never crossed your mind. But I would bet you've seen my work: it has been broadcast everywhere, on most of the news channels worldwide.*

That year I was working in Jordan as a human rights advocate, researching a report that required me to gather witness testimony from Yazidis, Mandaeans, Assyrians and other religious, ethnic and linguistic minority communities forced to flee Al Qaeda's extreme violence. Hundreds of thousands had sought scattered refuge: first in Jordan, Lebanon and Syria, and then they were granted it in various (but with some notable exceptions, fairly low) numbers across the Western world.[152] So the story struck me particularly – Kureishi's style, always dark but deeply humane, asks 'you' to confront who gawps, and what you gawp at, even as you read, dread mounting. It tests where your own choices for empathy might take you, and shows you where they end. As the narrator worries over the best angle to film such awful violence, the story writes in creative doubt, the ego of the artist making the work. Its sensibility equally indicts Western news 'values'; the foreign reporters who, the narrator implies, distance themselves from suffering and death while electing to *cover* Iraq.

If this work would speak to any seam of the years that followed, it was a warning of the infinite, absurd and horrific ambiguities the *war on terror* would cause. *We are innocent;* the narrator says of himself, his fellow civilian Iraqis, even as his unidentified bosses knock at the door: time to film another job. What are the terms of engagement with the character, and what is the point of recognition here? What is culpability? Though neither Hamid's nor Kureishi's narrators *actually admit to* committing violence, if the stories had them caught by the British or American forces, and locked up – would you meet them with empathy, say, years later, say, in a high-security prison on an American-owned island, or somewhere under a wind-farm in the English Fens?

Maybe they wouldn't make it. Sunjeev Sahota's novel, *Ours Are the Streets*, was also published in 2011, the year the Prevent strategy began. It is epistolary, its *you* is diffused as young university graduate, Imtiaz Raina, a British Pakistani Muslim from post-industrial Sheffield, writes to his dead father, and to his young, white wife from whom he is estranged, and to his baby daughter, Noor. To himself, or to you, however you find him.

And now the story swerves into our territory, into the *homegrown*. Imtiaz is the son of a taxi driver. He becomes radicalised into violence when he visits Pakistan to scatter his father's ashes. His cousins take him to Afghanistan and Kashmir, he learns his history and the history of Imperial and Indian oppression there. He returns to Sheffield, not to his old life, but to fulfil his destiny as a suicide bomber.

Sahota, who was born in Britain with Indian origins writes the horrific future: the working-class bind, the psychological split, manageable up to a point of crisis; the awakening to Western militaristic damage, the questions of home, forever unaddressed. There is a heart-stopping moment where the former local youth / jihadi in training lies to a white saviour in Pakistan saying (effectively) *he aint no terrorist.* This is another Booker-longlisted novel, though a critic found its flaw to be in the gap between thought and deed – the actual machinery and lure of radicalisation – the fall to ideology and from there to violence, judged as ineffectively portrayed in the character's arc (a charge that also might be levelled at Hamid's novel). But the issue is not whether it is the role or responsibility of South Asian / British / Muslim writers to explain (in fiction) how radicalisation operates theologically. The question is: why do we know so little about why and how the algorithm of radicalisation works so compellingly in our current systems, from online technology, through school and media and on human minds at all, despite all the policing, protection and surveillance we have?

THE PRISON INSIDE THE PRISON

Writing exercise: any life experience can make interesting fiction

To write about our memories, we need safe housing. The writers want to learn how to work with the past without dumping information on their readers. So she teaches a bit of Proust, because why not? She teaches a basic madeleine. A cake not many of the students know is still a cake. We play a game of cake-related word association – the feelings cake evokes are universal in the room.

Now imagine she adds half an hour on the ordering of chaos via the technical difficulty of Haiku. Not everyone knows *syllables* but everyone understands *beats*. And everyone can count 5-7-5.

Task 1: Think of a food you love, and which you associate with childhood. Write three lines. The last should capture the emotion of the first two, and no actual naming of a feeling is allowed. Include a seasonal reference. Follow the Haiku form.

The puzzle of the work seems absorbing. The challenge is a mind game with beauty as result. After an hour, the class has 20 food memories as Haiku. We share them. The room becomes full, as we are all also hungry. There is lamb biryani, there are Eccles cakes, there is Scotts porridge and her own piece goes –

Aloo paratha
Made on Sundays by my Ma
Winter light, ghee smoke…

Task 2: Now consider this short excerpt. The book is semi-autobiographical; the narrator is standing in a prison line, waiting to use the phone. He is first-person bored, impatient, scathing, rude about the forced protocol of sharing; his descriptions of his fellow inmates go down well with her students, sparking banter and imagination. It is an example of how to fictionalise the everyday moments of any kind of life – that all these moments have a place in writing. The men had also often wondered aloud   whether a voice and a space in literature could be claimed by someone contemporary with direct experience of prison: here was one.

Now she inserts her food haiku in the middle of the extract. As a way of showing how to work with the past. So its all *fuck this*, and *bastard* that; the men in line stink of sweat, disinfectant and dirt and a lack of basic supplies. It's a loud place: shouts, metallic noises, slang traded, the soundscape of prison written as immersion; affect. The narrator is waiting, someone is smoking a tab and the smoke hangs pungent in the air. He closes his eyes (briefly) and tastes *aloo paratha, made on Sundays by his Ma. Winter light, ghee smoke.* Then the smoker pushes him forward and curses, *Move on, mate. For fucks' sake, get a move on.* They're both waiting to use the shared prison phone to call their solicitors. Neither has spoken to his mother for five or more years.

Task 3: Everyone in the class think of the most boring task you do. Take your time and using the extract as an example, write a short description, no frills. Teeth brushing. Music practice. Waiting outside on dark, cold mornings for a puppy to take a piss. Insert your food memory haiku somewhere into your description. And edit it, smooth it out.

Suddenly, they are all a bunch of essayists, working in back story, techniquing arcs of character. A prison-roomful of Prousts, searching, doing, finding, lost time.

At the end of the session, she takes the writing in. There's a piece about the everyday slime and stench of skinning mass produced chicken thighs in the prison kitchen, how it clings to your hands and segues into a memory of licking fingers fried chicken shop deliciousness in East London with the crew then a siren goes by and it's alarming and brings you back to the lunch bell, ringing inside. People liked the piece, and told the writer so. For what it is, it matters. It raises feeling and passes some hours, that's all.

Another day she comes up against the difficulty of school. A young man sits with his arms crossed, until she comes and sits with him. Painfully, slowly, he writes about how his father beat him for not being able to read and write in a classroom. Shame at home, and under the teacher's eye. She knows what he is inside for and struggles with it   as he tries to write   she thinks about what people call *do gooding*, or naïve. Whatever is said or not said in prison, there is nothing but reality here. So the moments of joy matter as much as the knowledge that for some

Every. Single. Word. Is a struggle. There's only, maybe, fifteen on the page. There's only respite in finishing it, and only for a while among the collective effort in the writing room. Know shame; turn away from it or towards it: a choice every man makes.

Researchers say that many on long and life sentences encounter deep shame in themselves early on in prison as they try to come to terms with their tariff, with what they have lost, and to come to an acceptance of what they have done, that it was possible for them to have done it.[153]

And prison itself is built to be psychotically, not only psychologically dislocating, which is another way of saying it's built to shame. She, not carrying keys, experienced the geography of the place as carceral in the sense of being led through the maze. That's part of the point of it, after all: we don't need Foucault to walk the long corridors and feel their effect on us before it becomes the internal map of our place in this world, right here.

A few hours every two weeks of creative writing over the course of one semester might hold all of this on pause; pushing inside towards making something others will hear, accept, enjoy. Rare times. This class can only stand next to each student, if it's possible, for a while. It offers a space for concentration away from the circumstances, for self-reflection, and for self-expression (which is not always shared with the group.) It is a reckoning, even when it's just a funny made-up story. It's painful, hopeful, spontaneous and while it is happening, it is all that matters.

The grip of the pen, the frown over the paper. The strange adrenaline of making a mark: the flight of the alone to the alone.

Today she's going over the difference between metaphor and simile: *she is a lion. She is like a lion. Rumi, someone offers. Do you know the poet? Lion of the heart.* She's aware of the ghosts in the room. She's aware of the nature of lions and humans and the uncanny space of this teaching. The splitting here from the other worlds that prison is. Outside the door, the quiet ones might become posturing, persuasive, abusive, *radicalisers*. The loud ones might bake the class cakes. This writing place is not for humanizing: it is instead as true to fiction's real potential: more human in its holding of complexity than most other spaces ever are. It's a risk. There is nothing here but possibility. There's nothing here but the way we write our stories. Say it again. Radical trust.

Someone wants to write in his mother tongue. We place his languages side by side. Then rearrange italics. Does it matter anymore, on a long, or life sentence, that he was once a young child soldier and then a refugee, then a gang member, then _____ to this? *Like desire, language disrupts, refuses to be contained within boundaries. It speaks itself against our will, in words and thoughts that intrude, even violate the most private spaces of mind and body,*[154] hooks writes.

She knows what it is like for her to leave. She wonders what it's like for the prisoner-students. To return after class, to the cell. One of them tells her, over tea in plastic cups and prison-made cake, that every hour, he's woken up by the guards, all night. It's a story he may have borrowed, or overheard, as trauma becomes collective. It also may happen to him. He probably has been warned not to tell it   especially not in this room

There is a place in this prison called the CSC – the Close Supervision Centre. The prison within the prison. The oubliette. Few people on the outside world know this place exists. Solitary within solitary. How long can a human mind and body endure it? What would it be like to come out of that, and into class? This place is the heart of darkness.

A friend, a criminologist writes to me:

They are dark spaces in more than one sense of the term, and they are certainly the terminus of the prison system. Physically, they are absolutely oppressive – the one I visited was tomb-like, a tiny cramped building within another 18m concrete wall within one of those huge fences tucked in the corner of Whitemoor's 18m perimeter wall. What I also remember was that the sun was overhead but it was very cold at noon on a blazing day in late June 2019. It seemed that the CSC maybe got an hour or two of midday sun near the solstice, but no more. All the walls were damp and had lichen on the slabs and moss in the cracks, the way caves and rock overhangs do.[155]

Where did this darkness rise from? British prisons are where its worst viciousness refracts, disperses, concentrates Imperialism's long shadow in the figure of Earl Mountbatten of Burma, uncle of the current Duke of Edinburgh, the husband of the Queen.) In 1947, he, last Viceroy of India, oversaw Partition. In 1966, home now, he headed the *Report of the Inquiry into Prison Escapes and Security* on the implementation of *treatment and rehabilitation* of British prisoners. He set the system for categorisation of prisoners into A, B, C and D, with prisons to match, where A is the *worst*. He also proposed a fortress Guantánamo-style prison be built on the Isle of Wight, off the coast of England, where today, a disused prison is being considered by Priti Patel to be a suitably out of sight and out of mind location to *house* (intern, incarcerate) asylum seekers.[156]

Instead of Mountbatten's supermax idea, Category A prisoners were *dispersed* among *less dangerous* men to dilute the *control problems* they posed. This meant sending them to designated dispersal prisons. Whitemoor was one such prison, built on a former rail freight yard in the early 1990s.

CSCs superseded the *special security* units that existed for IRA prisoners from the early 90s onwards. Some CSCs occupied the same spaces. They were meant to contain Category A prisoners in seven places including Whitemoor. A friend notes:

> *It is thought that they are not routinely used for men convicted of terrorism offences; instead, a significant number of those living in them are there because they have killed or tried to kill other prisoners or members of staff, have taken hostages, or are believed to have made organised and coordinated attempts to escape.*[157]

The terminus is here. What to do with someone in your care who might harm or kill someone in your care?

In 1979, Mountbatten was lobster fishing on his Irish estate. He was killed by a targeted IRA bomb, *to bring attention to the British occupation*, the *terrorists* said. In 2016, the Conservative government revisited his early idea with a plan to create one supermax prison for *terrorists*[158]   the word echoes through the ages where the Irish used to be

She does not know if any in her room have seen the inside of this place, although she knows that incarcerated men have described it as a *torture unit*.[159] The UN has agreed.[160] She imagines that when you are down there, all you can do is pray.

Tea break ends and they begin again.

To write of memories, to speak of trauma. Not to have lost the way to do that. And have it be read. Such work might need strong boundaries   as no border force   could ever make   such work surely needs safe housing.

A SINGULARLY TALENTED, WILDLY IMAGINATIVE DEBUT NOVELIST

It's Fall 2018. I am sitting in the corner office of a shining tower just a short walk from Central Park, Manhattan. On the other side of the beautiful, busy desk of Sonny Mehta, then Editor in Chief at Knopf, at Penguin Random House. He is smoking, framed by a wall of the books he has published, from *American Psycho* to *A Thousand Acres* the shelves behind him stuffed with postcards and memorabilia, jackets under consideration, galleys he was working on.

He had just published my first novel, and this was towards the end of my trip to promote it in America. I had travelled across the country, and taken out time to explore California. I had seen the standing dead – the charred ghosts of trees turned carbon needles by vast forest fires that had swept the state that year and would come again. I had gone to coastal bookshops, and libraries and lighthouses, and met so many people, listening to stories at bar counters and in nail bars. Sonny wanted to hear all about it. In the airports, on the trains, in the hotel restaurants there was only one subject people were discussing. Christine Blasey Ford's testimony, Brett Kavanaugh's nomination to the Supreme Court. The heart and the voice: the question of justice. The #MeToo movement rising

For the first time in my life I had been homesick: for what I could not say. Sonny knew: the atro-city makes it easy for some to travel downwards. Makes it hard to hold your ground when you come up. He acknowledged the feeling with a silence. Then he asked me what I might work on next. A classic atro-city move. I did not yet fully know, and changed the subject, thinking about prison, the writing workshop at HMP Whitemoor I was returning to teach.

Around the same time, Knopf had published another debut novel. The hardcover jacket was red with a skull made of tiny white guns and stars. *Cherry* is a semi-autographical story by a man who was incarcerated in 2012, when he was 19 years old. He got 11 years, but was released early, on parole licence in October, 2019. Nico Walker, decorated Iraq veteran, former drug addict, PTSD suffering, bank robber. His main character is not violent – *One thing about holding up banks is that you are mostly robbing women, so you don't ever want to be rude. About 80 per cent of the time, so long as you're not rude, the women don't mind when you hold up the bank, probably it breaks up the monotony for them.*[161] Nico Walker, well-schooled, fiction writer. I told Sonny I was thinking about his novel, how it came to the world. We talked about my seminars. In many ways it was a surreal conversation, as being around Sonny always felt. It was a long way from the prison workshop to that office, and he knew that.

Back then, Walker was still incarcerated. I asked if I could somehow meet him. I was more interested in talking to someone who might remind me of my *real* life than sharing notes on Knopf marketing strategy (which, for *Cherry*, didn't mention any of Walker's biography on the hard cover jacket; he was billed only as a singularly talented, wildly imaginative debut novelist). It would be too difficult to get the permissions, Sonny said. He gave me the novel as we were leaving for lunch.

In many ways Walker's own story is the dream for many, not least men in prison, writing. For the publishing industry, bank robbery was more or less palatable, offset in the press by the 'war hero' status, expressed in the novel through his narrator's depiction of *hajis*, of shooting up heroin and Iraqis, the years he didn't sleep for dreaming of the desert and blood. Iraq here, Iraq there. Iraq: the war as event that happens and happens and happens. Walker recalls: *It was just, like, go out there and piss these people off until somebody shoots at you or blows something up. And then go fuck some more shit up until they do it again. We were literally there to create conflict so they could report on it at home, and justify more fucking spending.*[162] The war is what gave Walker his PTSD, with the heroin addiction as a reward when he got home. Bank robbing for drugs landed him in medium security where someone tried to stab him with a pencil shank as he taught the GED algebra class. Put it this way – it was hard enough.

He was supported in his writing and his publishing journey by Giancarlo DiTrapano, publisher of Tyrant Books, who took an interest in him, and told him, *The only way you're gonna get out of the shadow of your own fucking life is to write this out.*[163] The result, after years of work and false starts was *a major book deal*, a *New York Times* bestseller, a million dollar movie adaptation. By the time you read this, *Cherry,* the film, will already be out, Walker is engaged to poet, columnist and former sex worker Rachel Rabbit White, he borrows her eyeliner, they will have lived for a while in Mississippi according to the terms of his parole. The book parties have been wild, naked, drugged up *conjunctions of eight different micro niche literary world types*[164]

Yet to read this novel in 2018 is to think about the violence of othering, of dissociative culture and what it does to a white man; and what it makes white men do in a far-off desert war, and sitting in Sonny's office I remember my mind sliding to the bite of the pale, lost TA boys I kissed in my hometown when I was young, the makeup of the English newsroom on 9/11, little knowing or caring of the basic difference between Sunni and Shi'a (and Sufi); the gates and gates of Whitemoor prison and the men I know there. *I think about going to the Co-op to buy pre-sliced carrot sticks and apples and passing the censor with humous and dips and extracts of novels in my bag. It's always cold when we arrive at the prison gates, its always dark when we leave.*

Thinking about that, and dangerous, murderous harm, while going down in the elevator, and walking slowly, at Sonny's pace across Broadway on a fresh fall day in post 9/11

New York, and about war, and PTSD, and bank robbing, and drug abuse, and terror and writing and prison. A certain form of a dream literary lunch now follows: French menus and wine and long conversations with a famously silent man: patron saint of outsiders / a culture-maker, holding his own through the atro-city. Navigating *culpability* while embodying power but always with a certain radical edge. We talk about New York water tanks and pre-Independence Indian art; about good reviews and bad reviewers, when *and how* to choose to speak against power   about *the terms* of survival and the nature of struggle vs. *money*

It was one of the last times I saw him before I returned to England. He died a little over a year later, on December 30, 2019. When this (my eventual *next book*) existed as no more than a handful of pages about terror and trauma, the first three weeks of complex racial grief, and loss.

The risks of writing might be difficult, vertiginous. To *fail* or *succeed* might precipitate a displacement, even erasure of self. A certain kind of death. It might be sublime, as *spice*   as a drug

THE QUESTION OF HEALING

As a young woman she read Judith Lewis Herman's seminal work, *Trauma and Recovery*. Which thinks through the transmuting symptoms of PTSD across traumas – from being in a war, to being severely and racially bullied in the classroom, to being sexually abused – it manifests in some as the need for control, for constant social approval, or the lack of ability to take responsibility or accept criticism on any small thing. PTSD as profoundly arrested development. The maddening constant prison noise or the intensity of solitary segregation feed these – she knows that prison is a place of alienating, brutalising sensory deprivation that exacerbates feelings and experiences of shame, oppression, indignity and injustice sometimes beyond suppressible reason. Not so much *post* as repeating traumatic stress syndrome. The kindness or commitment of individuals, the education programme that offers time to step away from the past into a present and might promise a future of making something, anything, with others, matters in the moment that it happens, because it must. It brings so much, to many. But creative writing is a risk   she tries to say   it holds its own potential in the form   her tools for safety are asking for small classes, a panopticon of the whole prison, because   context is everything   what comes into the room   she needs to keep the students safe   she asks power   for life stories nothing is forthcoming from above.   She focuses on craft to deconstruct hierarchies   never praise the finished piece   only the doing of work.   In her prison writing class, the origin of harm or the inflicting of it, the deeper impacts of PTSD won't make themselves easily known. Have you ever made a space for creativity   and taught it to   a room of people where half of them are trying to breathe without exhaling, because it is not allowed? And the other half are trying to create the conditions for exhalation even though they are struggling with all their unspoken questions, especially the ones they are not allowed to ask? Into that silence, *writers* are working   and the prison seems to the governor to become *a different place*

It is difficult to write this as Palestine is eradicated under Israeli fire. As Kashmir suffers yet more Hindutva violence, all of this made so much worse by capitalism where it meets the Covid pandemic. As the new Brexit-inflamed border policies in Northern Ireland incite riots after decades of relative peace, partitions are felt in their iterations, more cousins and brothers and sisters of children in Belfast and Bradford, Birmingham, Cobridge, Cambridge, Manchester, London, all watching, and everyone else wondering *what has this to do with me? Perhaps hoping nothing, perhaps remembering*

The images from Northern Ireland spark something half understood in a 1980s childhood, when the IRA were that decade's *terrorists,* the hardcore population of the prison system. There are still bright, Irish, highly motivated youth, good at school, determined to prove they are 'on the right track' inside English cells. Category A's most unifying identity, its most potent drug might be intergenerational, osmotic PTSD.

There were a few ex-soldiers of one kind or another in her class. As ex-military, trained in combat with high levels of self-control, self-motivation; a determination to succeed in public, and be seen as a perfect this or that, might just be high-pressure upbringing. It might be keeping a person alive, and then there is the new iteration

Iraq here, Iraq there. In terms of war in the Middle East and its long aftermath, she does not forget Gulf War Syndrome, a collection of symptoms suffered by returning war veterans in Britain and America from the Gulf in 1990-91. Fatigue, chronic pain, insomnia, muscle aches. Sounds like PTSD, though it apparently is not (which is equally concerning). 250,000 returning American troops were diagnosed with it; few were treated. Among the fascist insurgents who stormed the American capitol in 2021 were Iraq and Afghanistan vets; now on the frontline of what they perceive as a civil war against *radicals* undermining borders, values, claim to resources – their targets Black Lives Matter, democrats; any others they call *threat*.[165]

In UK prisons, rates of PTSD are higher than in the general population, and that's true of staff and of residents.

Education offers a respite, and meaningful activity over time. Productivity for its own sake, not for sale. The place of art in this is something to think about. Respite, perhaps. A portal. A chance to build incremental moments of self esteem against the state's efficient machinery. It cannot be done alone. Art offers a different kind of holding position there.

But if the problem art poses is that it signifies little about the maker except the capacity to make art, and that can't be read as a sign of *goodness*, then something else is needed overall. Now she starts dreaming of different possibilities and worlds; a way not to have the question of what 'art' is be consistently considered answered as *a good, as a luxury*, but instead consider it an essential part of human development; and of an equal society; in which it carries no burden but as one click among many interlocking systems that turn from violence, punishment, shame.

Think of this as *Outline* instead (where *Aftermath* is the feminist's principle of autobiographical writing). *A novelist teaching a course in Creative Writing* over three years of winters in Cambridgeshire. Takes her College students in a mini-bus across the flat lands to the high-security prison. The young people are coming to the prison to practice creative writing alongside incarcerated men. *She leads her students in storytelling exercises.* They *speak* about themselves: carefully, sometimes directly, sometimes metaphorically, about their *anxieties*, *pet theories, regrets and longings.* They write, together. And through these disclosures, *a portrait of* a group *is drawn by contrast* holding trust against *great loss*, and there is more to come.[166] We will all learn ourselves, the complexity of this world, practicing our fictions there.

In the last days of December 2019, some of the men who were in her Whitemoor class wrote to her. They expressed their shock and disbelief at the attack at Fishmongers' Hall. Their letters were full of care. Some had been placed on indefinite sentences for public protection, life without parole. Some were in under joint enterprise, and some for terrorist related offences.

She remembers the incarcerated man who began to write to his estranged brother after having taken her course. Turns out the brother had dreams of becoming a writer too, and they began to swap life stories.

THOSE WHO LEAVE, THOSE WHO STAY

The writer Tayari Jones knows that the child of the incarcerated parent knows disenfranchised grief. That the parent of the incarcerated child knows disenfranchised grief. That the victim's family knows violence, and grief. That the perpetrator's family knows the void, their pain as unspeakable as the crime: as violation. She knows that to survive prison, there is an argument for writing. There is an argument for writing about that writing, not only about prison.

In her novel *An American Marriage*, a man, Roy is wrongfully convicted of rape. We do not read the event or the trial. He is sent to prison, where he and his newlywed wife Celestial write letters to each other throughout his long sentence. Roy and Celestial are Black, the embodiment of the American Dream and the New South. Roy is arrested just as they are becoming *white rich*. Police come for him: take him from their bed in a raid on their home in the night.

Roy learns to survive: he meets his estranged, long-absent father inside.

Roy is eventually released.

Celestial has become a successful artist by making dolls of him, highlighting his case. But on his return Roy finds she has not waited for him. She loves another living man: Roy's former friend Andre. Love: an elastic band stretched almost to wire, reforms misshapen. Roy teeters on the edge of violence. A reckoning happens, laced with the threat and the longing to go back to prison. Celestial, disenfranchised so many times over, sacrifices her new life for Roy and what happens to her? A different kind of solitary looms

When Tayari Jones was a child a white serial killer targeted Black children in her hometown of Atlanta. Twenty eight were killed. She knew two of them. She became a teacher and published two novels. Still, she struggled to maintain a writing career working against odds of all kinds. So many women writers of colour have a version of this story. The reading room shelf holds few like her. The numbers do not lie.

The year *An American Marriage* is published in the UK, I am invited to sit on the jury for a national literary prize. It's the first time I have done this work. I'm in the revolving chair: there are also two prize jury veterans. We are having a conversation about the suspension of disbelief. There's another 'prison novel' under consideration by a voice more tuned to their ears. The story includes a high-stakes escape from *maximum-security*. One of the judges sees this plot twist as more convincing than a

Black American man meeting his long-estranged father inside.

The day before this discussion, I had been teaching in Whitemoor. My mind folds as lives touch each other, meet each other, and I hear my voice trying to insist, to explain to this jury – the doctrine of *joint enterprise*, how *dispersal* works, how the system might well produce such a moment of relation. That Black men who know each other might meet inside more regularly than a woman prisoner making an *escape*. I think about how Black women's authority is regarded in my country, and all that is never said. I make the point: the revolving chair begins to turn. *I am allowed to win the battle, not the war.* The long, not the shortlist.

Tayari Jones asks before the fact, and years before the far right Capitol *insurgency* in 2021, *Let's say Trump is not re-elected. Let's say all over the world, these far-right regimes are put down. How will we live with our neighbours, knowing what we now know of them?*

Racial grief: the heartsickening trauma of a long history of policy-driven shame and human counternarrative, is Jones' core subject. The grief of knowing neighbours who cannot step up for each other, all the way through to wider culture, which, in the UK now seeks to legally silence protest, demand voter registration ID, arrest or refer to Prevent those who publicly express solidarity for the Palestinian people. As I write, the Police, Crime and Sentencing Bill seeks to expand the Home Secretary's powers, via police to contain and punish, to extend sentences[167]   the grief is so heavy, it is meant to imprison us, if not even stop us dead. The literary has a responsibility in this, as a joint enterprise, as culture is made and protected by many.

An American Marriage gives its readers the gift of an intimate voice and specific portrait of two lives to think about this grief. It is not the insider-view of the system or prison but about the damage that conviction, the shame that silence, that the culture of it does to families of those convicted. From the core to the widest sense. It's risky. It's a subject rarely spoken of. The horror of crime usually elides all deserving of story. Jones says, *This is the story about a family affected by wrongful conviction, about what they owe each other and the ways that they will move forward. I think that when we forget that part of stories, we are actually dismantling community.*[168]

And yet though the novel makes the strong suggestion, it never definitively answers the question of whether Roy is guilty or not. Jones trades in narrative as radical doubt. She as writer believes Roy is innocent: she presents us with the choice of whether we can believe this ourselves. Roy says he is innocent. His mother believes him. He pleads with Celestine to try. It has to be enough.

In this way Jones welcomes us to trust her, and her characters and to grieve with them, and with her. She invites us to sit, as a visitor to a prison, with our own flawed selves: our radical doubt and our potential for trust, lets go so far as to say *hope*

A voice says, will always say – *there is still the question of violence.* There will always be some who should be locked away. The storyteller, to avoid that violation will not go there without backstory – to help us understand. There is still the question of real life

When Tayari Jones comes to Britain, she says her concern spreads beyond clear miscarriages of justice to encompass the vast numbers of those in jail for non-violent drug offences, or who are mentally ill. *I'm not only interested in the 'innocent people'* she says. *When we make that distinction between innocent and not innocent, we miss the major issues about prison reform.*[169] I wonder about those two statements – the *non violent* and the *mentally ill* – locked uneasily together. There's no space to consider what is lost in the juxtaposition (or prison *reform* versus abolition). *Mentally ill* requires state money, requires commitment to racial justice. Requires a whole, honest education, to drill down to that belief in basic equality of potential. Meanwhile, though her fiction gives us a wrongfully convicted man, Jones's statement encompasses violent offenders. I even wonder if she said those words, but they did not survive the editor's cut.

There is nothing to move forward with but doubt; and that might mean listening to the subtext, listening harder to lived reality as well as our own hopes. The novel almost ends with this sentence (that pun, again) in recognition of life

Neither of us closed our eyes against the immeasurable dark of that silent night[170]

What keeps me awake after reading *An American Marriage* is Jones' clarity on the price that everyone harmed by structural violence pays and continues to pay. Which is all of us. And the incredulity of having to sit on a literary jury and answer the question with a killjoy's experience, when what they hungered for was people as numbers   as facts   as if that would make them *feel*

How likely is it that a Black man might meet a relative in prison?

REALITY HUNGER AS JOINT ENTERPRISE
(A KILLJOY MANIFESTO)[171]

A killjoy manifesto thus begins by recognising inequalities as existing.[172]

Where are their *mothers*? (Tut tut.) She reads in the newspaper, and it as if she has always known that Black women are four times more likely to die in childbirth than white women in the UK.[173] That British Pakistani (read *working class*) women are more likely to have a premature baby or neonatal death in the UK compared to their country of origin.[174] That Asian women are twice as likely to die in childbirth than white women in the UK.[175]   That mental health never *falters* in South Asian *communities*   that Black African, black Caribbean, Bangladeshi and Pakistani women were nearly twice as likely as white women to have died with Covid-19. The fact is not linked to health.[176]

She learns from her students that joint enterprise is a common law doctrine where an individual can be jointly convicted of the crime of another, if the court decides they *foresaw* that the other party was likely to commit that crime. It is guilty by knowing someone's mind   guilty by association   sometimes just standing there

Young men from black, Asian and minority ethnic (BAME) groups have been disproportionately affected or explicitly targeted by joint enterprise convictions in cases of presumed gang-related violence[177]

She confronts this truth each time she enters the prison. She asks the class to write a piece in response to a NASA image of a spaceman, floating in zero gravity, in the starry void. One comes back – *Is he on his own or is he with a friend?*[178]

She has to keep making the same claim because she keeps countering the claim that what she says exists does not exist.[179]

As thrusters boost away from space,
And being lost forever.[180]

She is being bombarded with splintering statistics that feed the curation of the *homegrown* student, lecturer, professor demographic in elite universities[181]

No dream, just stuck in my own thoughts, but I am lonely.[182]

Her friends joke and she begins to repeat the joke that she *is the darkness.* She remembers that *if a killjoy manifesto shows how the denial of inequality under the assumption of equality is a technique of power, then the principles articulated in that manifesto cannot be abstracted from statements about what exists.*[183]

She reads of the cells, and how they change your eyesight, make you see differently – *20/20 vision oops, yeah there's a lizard*[184]

She discovers that at least one man in her class was convicted on joint enterprise. For murder, though he was not holding the knife and did not know it was there. At 20, he got a minimum sentence of 19 years. He has autism. She is told only   that he has *difficulty concentrating.* All she knows of him is in her classroom. Where he works with deep concentration through every class, and supports others, more than many do.[185]

Despite having dyslexia, he continues, *there was no help… you were left to your own devices… there was no interest.*[186]   He lives to make *the story* widely known

She wants to say, *In our society, for a whole lot of people, getting sent to jail is not something out of the ordinary or unexpected, rather it is a part of their lives.*[187]

In a 2016 ruling, R v Jogee, the Supreme Court ruled that joint enterprise had been misinterpreted for the past 30 years.

Hundreds convicted before that date remain incarcerated

A killjoy manifesto is thus about making manifest what exists.[188]

She thinks about *Antigone*, the power of canonical metaphor, and of myth. The devising of an EPIC scale to be used to evaluate students' experience of learning.[189]

59 per cent of prisoners stated that they had regularly played truant from school, 63 per cent had been suspended or temporarily excluded, and 42 per cent stated that they had been permanently excluded or expelled. *Prisoners with these issues were more likely to be reconvicted on release than those without.*[190]

In prison she hears the lament as refrain:
I have been a stranger here in my own land
All my life[191]

She is aware of the issues. Radicalisation, release, recidivism. And then remembers that the number of Muslims in prison has increased by almost 50 per cent over the last decade from 8,900 to 13,200. Muslims now make up 15 per cent of the prison population, but just 5 per cent of the general population [...] It must be stated and stated that this dramatic rise in the number of prisoners is not linked to terrorism offences, as on average, very few people are convicted of these offences each year.[192]

I'm so far but yet so near wishing on a star wishing you were here.[193]

It is argued that in many such cases [of joint enterprise] the level of participation in the offence was so slight, or the evidential threshold of conviction so low, that the conviction amounts to a substantial injustice.

He has no control. He has no power over destiny. He can only let go and allow fate to take him.[194]

Prosecution teams were reported as being more likely to appropriate discourses of *gang insignia* and music videos or lyrics, particularly hip hop and rap genres, as a way of building a JE [joint enterprise] case against BAME prisoners.[195]

trap trap in the bando I don't wanna look like you[196]

Disclaimer: the artist / artists would like to clarify no persons in my music, mixtape videos are in anyway involved or condone any illegal activities as portrayed in the lyrics or contents of any video or song produced.[197]

Genre is a medium security prison[198]

This chain which now you wear so openly:
Beside the charge, the shame, imprisonment[199]

37 per cent of prisoners reported having family members who had been convicted of a non-motoring criminal offence, of whom 84 per cent had been in prison, a young offenders' institution or borstal.[200]

Do you think a young Muslim man could meet or make a friend or brother or a son in a UK prison?[201]

People in prison had called him Roy's pops, but he'd just assumed it was a joke.[202]

You can't pick your home any more than you can choose your family. In poker you get five cards. Three of them you can swap out, but two are yours to keep: family and native land.[203]

I cannot tell whether he is ascending or descending. Is he suspended in a vacuum of time?[204]

The feminist killjoy is a manifesto. *She is assembled around violence; how she comes to matter, to mean, is how she exposes violence.*[205]

I'm not there or should I say here but where is here cos I'm in the middle of nowhere alone with my thoughts.[206]

Prisoners with a convicted family member were more likely to be reconvicted in the year after release from custody than those without a convicted family member.[207]

You hold yourself aslant, the tip of your own hemisphere, a circumference hole and entire, above clouds and horizons and ozone layers.[208]

At least two generations have been disciplined to expect (and receive) little or nothing from the state except punishment or the threat of punishment.[209]

In Search of Lost Time is the narrative of a desire to write[210]

The impact on the students was profound.[211]

All she can get back to now is this: *Society's collective fear of love must be faced if we are to lay claim to a love ethic that can inspire us and give us the courage to make necessary changes.*[212]

No, I did not describe the mirror — I was the mirror. And the words they are themselves, without a discursive tone.[213]

ANTIGONE'S LAMENT

I never taught *Antigone* in the prison. There was no reason not to. Maybe such stories take their truest form within these walls. (Ismene is convicted under joint enterprise, after all.) Which raises the question of what to teach in prison, and why. What kind of city we might make. *It is not a city if it takes its orders from one voice.* There's another line, which sounds a warning: *How about you, in a public brawl with justice?* And the response comes back, *There is no threat in speaking to emptiness.*

All I want now is to gather up the fragments. To make safe what was never safe. The only thing to do is to tell the whole truth. *I am sorry you prefer silence. I have been stranger here in my own land   All my life.* I knew   passing   but did not *know* how much damage it could mean. The metaphor breaks down. *Neither love, nor lamentation, no song but silence.* This is no myth. There is only a city that cannot be made safer by building over its cracks. There is only a group of young students, who remember what they experienced. Years pass. Thinking of the many still in prison. Thinking of what the future might bring to all of them.

There is nothing written   there is   no such thing as fate. I cannot think much more about the knot of history, fiction and our lived, much harsher sentences. I can only pass on this story. These cryptic words in this strange order. And wait for the fiction writer who might go further, as the reader might one day.

IN PRISON, THE LACK OF RESOURCES IMPROVES ONE'S CREATIVITY

It is early November 2019. Her writing seminar is now in its third year, the semester is almost done. She decides to set Ahmet Altan's *Voyage Around My Cell*, a chapter from his prison memoir, *I Will Never See The World Again,* in translation by Yasemin Çongar. Altan, the renowned Turkish writer and journalist, was arrested in 2016 on allegations of spreading *subliminal messages announcing a military coup*, on television. He was charged with attempting to overthrow the national order and interfering with the work of the national assembly and the government. He was given a life sentence in 2018 and subsequently tried on Turkey's terrorism charges, often used to convict high-profile people speaking against the state. He was finally released after three years.[214] He is the category of prison-writer people campaign for, listen to. The bona fide prisoner of the pen.

She knows that so much of what he has to say in this piece might have been written by one of the men she teaches. The description of the dimensions of the cell. An invitation in, to think about *place* as feeling. The question of hours locked down. An ability to think about *time* as a condition for reflection. The details of materiality: the plastic trestle table, the stackable chairs. A way to show how the objective correlative might work for difficult emotions. The things that become precious, when those are all there are.

The writing is mostly sparse, as prison itself. The students might also have something to say about the moving descriptions of abundance and scarcity, Altan's observation that in prison, the lack of resources improves one's creativity. It's something she has thought about before, in another discipline: how the monastic cell allows, even encourages the inner life to become consuming; how the writer craves solitude yet is constantly open to distractions, called *research* in this world. Writing seminars for beginners often start with a conversation about where ideas come from. The cells.

Altan muses about the value of writing as an exercise during incarceration. The possibility of forgetting about everything for a while, about prison itself; indignity. *Like all writers, I want both to forget and to be remembered,* Altan says. Here is the bind of this strange art, and perhaps of the prison writer's condition in the strange room. Altan writes:

> *I throw myself into unachievable dreams. Those are the dreams where I can alter time and space, where I can be in the century and the age of my choosing. It is a magical jungle filled with pleasure*

*and games. There I take life and mould it into a different shape
every day.*

This is the kind of freedom she thinks that these writers get
from those few hours spent writing together. With a group of
young students who make the journey from the heart of the
atro-city to what society considers its underworld, to work
alongside them. And the same happens to them. The writers
in her class of 2019 wrote their own, *Voyage Around My Cell*
pieces. All of them considered, crafted, fresh interpretations
on the theme. Some of the men argued with Altan. *He got it
wrong.* The cell can be *a solace*, one said, from the rest of the
prison; offering some kind of dignity when it is hard to hold to
inside oneself; even while a sentence lasts into years. Trying to
capture the sense of something, and release the joy of writing
in the capture: in form.

The prison courtyard here is quite sparse, she understands. In
Altan's piece, which contains some whimsy, (the kind rarely
expressed by her students,) courting birds drop pale flowers
on the prison yard as they fly overhead and the prisoners pick
them up and take them inside. *The next morning, the wardens
come in and take them away. Flowers are forbidden in the prison.*

Reading those words now, she is reminded of the last
time she saw Usman Khan. In the visitor's room at HMP
Whitemoor, in March 2018, at the end of course celebration
for that year's writing seminars. It was a bright day, at which

all the graduating writers read their work to guests, some with pride, some nervously. One reminded the audience, his voice shaking, that the last time he had read in front of a crowd, he had been in court.

Each student had been allowed to invite a guest. Friends, family members, University representatives and a Member of Parliament mingled with the men. Characteristic of the prison's faith in the education programme it was allowed that tulips could be brought in to decorate the tables of the meeting room. At the close of the day, everyone took a bunch, and offered stems to each other. As we left, visitors reclaimed the prisoners' flowers, and took them home with us.

EPILOGUE

I will never be able to fathom how any man can make the calculated choice to commit violence. Or ever fully know what happens in individual minds before, or in prison, or upon release. I am repeatedly stopped by the facts of this case: the confluence of experts', specialists' and authorities' best intentions / oversight / forensic insight / inexperience/ call it negligence / or blindness/ optimism bias/ struggle or hope.

The long aftermath of that day in London Bridge continues to be felt in its many spirals of grief. An inquest into the deaths of Jack and Saskia happens. It is difficult to hear many say that they are sorry for the loss, that changes will be made, but that they would not, even in retrospect have done anything differently, what can be said after that?

The atro-city is a labyrinth that forces us always to double back. Dead ends open to new avenues; avenues I thought open are a mirage. Towers of learning are built on voids. In isolation the voices fully whisper. Power tells a story to sustain itself, it has no empathy for those it harms   it washes its hands of them   and this is a catalyst. The performance of real feeling for your fellow humans is a dangerous state to live in.

Some days it seems that in the atro-city there is only

exploitation, extraction, capital, *reputation*. The repetition of events justifies the ends: as the *war on terror* has been described as *endless*, as hundreds more people will now endure more racist treatment in the UK's systems. As the threat level will remain very high.

Then lockdown. The pandemic has no morals: like fear, it thrives on our 'values,' the world we jointly make. In prison, people are being held in cells for 23 hours a day. Drugs and weapons get in, are made, somehow. Education slows or stops. Art and writing projects in this context may seem frivolous. They will take time to start again. Will that make anyone safer? In prison, an individual's sense of injustice or where they find political affinity, in violent ideology or in evangelical faith or adherence to some nationalism, cannot be made metaphor. The filling of time is a pressing concern. What happens in prison. Young men grow up, young women: the atro-city is waiting.

So the question of arts inside or outside prison is not a small one. It is not a frivolous one. There is a wounded sense of denial and resistance some feel about giving people who have committed harm such chances, when so many children, even perhaps their own, have had library and arts and social centres and cultural opportunities denied them and individual capital must fill the gap, as the state focuses on ever deeper policing. There is an obviousness to the cycle of value we are in, itself a constant state of traumatic stress disorder. The reckoning of whose life matters more has for generations been managed in Britain by saying – *look over there!* (insert: USA / France / the *teeming multitudes* of 'Africa' and India and Pakistan and Bangladesh and) *Look how bad they are!* The quality of education, the kind of access to art also matters: there is more to learn than what is given, there is nothing more to ask for than all of that at once. It is beyond time.

Then comes the formal lie. The Sewell Report was published in April 2021, one year after the global Black Lives Matter movement was fueled by the murder of George Floyd, the same week as the trial of the police who killed him began. The Commission on Race and Ethnic Disparities, set up by the conservative government who precipitated Brexit and the huge and disproportionate numbers of deaths of Black and Bangladeshi people in the UK during the Covid pandemic, found *no evidence of institutional racism* in Britain, and did what it meant to do: send whole communities into re-traumatised states. The UN decried the findings and was accused in turn by Patel of sowing division[215] – more radical activists were formed, I promise   while people will die from this

Abolition, in the widest sense and at the cellular level is a word, a world, a choice to make. A resonance to action. What else is there? Not *prison reform* or making prison more humane, long term. Not *redemption* with its echoes of the holy, except via art as incrementally: it might be restorative and so rehabilitative for a while, as any art making can be. At the very least it is proof of life. The question is – can it last in the world as we have it? The testimony of incarcerated men in Category

A facilities says – *doing this has given me back my sense of what I might be capable of – doing this has restored my sense of purpose* – we can hardly believe our eyes. I am reclaiming my trust in words while dreaming of that possible future right now. There is hope in it   as a means of survival.

True joy as non-violence is an instinct in us: it must be nurtured. It requires more from us than creative dreaming. It requires planning, organising in community. As Kaba writes, *I think that love is a requirement of principled struggle, both self love and love of others, that we must do all we can, that it is better to do something rather than nothing, that we have to trust others as well as ourselves.*[216] It is a risk I might take one day again. Whatever has happened, I have found my way back, in writing, to this certainty.

November 2020. Creative work keeps going alongside grief. I walk fifteen miles from a historic heart of the industrial revolution, where the Victorian tunnels are now a school child's living classroom, where remnants of coal and shipping across the empire are still felt in a shoreline still heavy with the leakage of tar into water. I arrive at the coast. I make spirals in sand, aware of the difference between doing this and capturing it in writing. Still in the maze of this draft text, I make a list of every body that we are meant to trust

     I wade into the sea

I realize the only body missing is my own. Here is my final arrival, the zenith of this *bildungsroman*. In the architecture of the atro-city I was considered the teacher, only there to deliver the sessions. But the privilege of teaching and of writing *fiction in this world* asks so much more of me. It has always meant insisting more, speaking up more, listening more   to different forms and lives   again and more. Trusting that instinct that says *we are not safe, something must change*, and saying it. Doing it. This time   needed more. Forgiveness for that betrayal of self   living with *what if*   will take a long time to find.   As might *new worlds* to forge.

We can sound sorrow but cannot end on it: now I follow the form. Even as, in sunlit corners, and on the steps of the Guildhall in Cambridge and on London Bridge, flowers are left for the memory of Jack Merritt and for Saskia Jones. New dishes are cooked in families, photographs are shared, poems weave voices together. Creativity marks, makes life. Loss in flux to rage and back to bittersweet: this event and its stories have such vast ramifications for so many. It will stand as a turning point among all the other paths a life could take.

The words that keep me in this world are only here; I leave them for everyone who falls to violent harms, out from the wreck towards some new imagined future where attempting to live with clarity in the struggle seems an everyday affair, as possible as it is necessary, after all. I know we cannot not lose any more. The atro-city cannot consume us. There is no time, no sentence that can contain. I am standing on the parapet with a lit match in one hand and a writer's love of dry paper. And then the flood.

Light changes under water, and through the refraction, the wreck might disappear. We do not want to make it anew. We need a different kind of ship to sail on a collective breath, taken and exhaled. Somewhere, an equal city is being written; it will spread

AUTHOR'S NOTE

This short book is about how a specific act of terrorist violence can shatter, rearrange and refocus us on what we have always known, what we think we know and what we choose to believe; and what narrative rushes into those gaps. It is about personal responsibility and identification in society, the phenomena of racial grief and personal loss, and generational trauma. About how to write with that. It is about fictions: as pervasive cultural myths and the harms they cause, about violence in many forms, about the terror we make and hold and what we lose to it. It's about safety, and about risk, about white saviourism, and about my teaching of fiction writing in prison – and writing fiction about terror and about prison. It's about radical doubt, and radical hope – especially *in the dark*, as Rebecca Solnit calls it. And finally about the fluid, shining faith not in a God or in the edicts of any organised religion or institution but in the necessary fiction we rest our contingent lives on, which in English we call *trust*.

The context of this book is British but it belongs in a global discourse of anti-racism and anti-capitalism: its politics rests on challenging myths of many kinds, and it is without borders. It is a small offering to the many who work and live tirelessly (though they do get overwhelmed and very, very tired) for the end of violent division and injustice in our world.

In the months of lockdown in 2020 when I was working on this book, in isolation and in an unfamiliar city, when thinking in coherent lines often felt like an achievement and writing almost impossible, the public speaking out against racism and on prison issues by David Merritt, his kindness and clarity kept me and countless others going when he and his family had so much to contend with. I am inspired by his example, and want to honour Jack and Saskia, whose wisdom and hope and actions made such a difference to so many.

The book is grounded in my long reading relationship with women poets, women of colour, Black feminist abolitionists, and it draws on the thinking of the many activists whose writing comes from both heartbreak and experience of state harms over decades. The works I reference offered ropes flung out over deep water. I am not a strong swimmer. I flailed between them; I didn't always catch them; that much is evident here and any errors are mine. I am grateful in particular to Arun Kundnani for his time and insights.

My deep thanks to Sabeena Akhtar, Gina Apostol, Adam Biles, Lucy Warwick Ching, Sarah Colvin, Pippa Crerar, Jeff Deutsch, Liz Dolman, Tina Gharavi, Lisa Ghiggini, Aisha K. Gill, Jodie Ginsburg, David Godwin, Rebecca Greene, Mark Haddon, Patrick Harbinson, Kristen Harrison, Alessandra Iervolino, Faisal Islam, Ben Jarman, Sweety Kapoor, Gitanjali Kumar, Naveen Kishore and all at Seagull Books, Tessa McWatt, Cécile Menon, Sandeep Parmar, Gitanjali Patel, Ayesha Ramachandran, Roz Ryan, Julie Sanders, Shuchi Saraswat, Rick Simonson, Paul Stanbridge, Pooja Taneja, Jeet Thayil, Laura Smith, and Margaret Wilkinson who made the kind of interventions that were life-saving, though they may not have known it at the time.

Learning Together was founded by Dr Ruth Armstrong and Dr Amy Ludlow at the University of Cambridge. It was delivered by a network of academics, educators and volunteers across the UK: it had a lasting and profoundly positive impact on so many people's lives. Those who taught the courses and participated in them from outside prison did so with great dedication and trust, as did many inside, across the prison estate. It was as demanding as it was humbling and inspiring to be in that writing room; working with Jack Merritt enhanced that immeasurably. I am continuously awed by the Cambridge student writing cohort of 2019-20, who go about their lives with such courage and commitment to social justice.

Above all, thanks to Adam Levy and Ashley Nelson Levy at Transit Books who invited me to write for Undelivered Lectures in 2018, then – having seen just a few pages of notes in early 2020 – took this for my contribution to the series on trust and stuck with it and me through the process. I'm grateful to Liza St. James and the whole Transit team for their attention to my work, and to Anna Morrison for the beautiful cover design.

My father, my sister and the Crowe family give so much love and support. My nieces and nephews always bring the important questions along with the joy.

Not a single day of my life for the last two decades, or a word of this book would have been possible without Ben Crowe and I dedicate it to him.

ENDNOTES

1.   'Dawn' in *The Collected Poems of Octavio Paz, 1957-1987*, Octavio Paz, trans. Eliot Weinberger (USA: New Directions, 1991), p.46.

2.   *Audre Lorde: Dream of Europe: Selected Seminars and Interviews*, 1984 –1992, ed. Mayra A. Rodriguez (Chicago: Kenning Editions, 2020), p.90.

3.   'The 10 Books I Needed to Write My Novel,' Ocean Vuong, *Literary Hub,* 1 October 2019, https://lithub.com/ocean-vuong-the-10-books-i-needed-to-write-my-novel/.

4.   *Audre Lorde: Dream of Europe,* ed. Mayra, p.77.

5.   *Racism, Islamophobia, Antisemitism: Othering and the Weakness of Christian Identity*, David Kline, panel discussion, Blavatnik School of Government, Oxford University, 14 April 2021, https://www.youtube.com/watch?v=f-Ba_x_jfxxY.

6.   *Living a Feminist Life*, Sara Ahmed (London: Duke University Press, 2017), p.14.

7.   All of this information can be found in the official transcripts for the inquests into the attacks: https://fishmongershallinquests.independent.gov.uk/.

8.   Learning Together is a national prisoner education programme based in the Institute of Criminology in the University of Cambridge. It was founded and run by Dr Ruth Armstrong and Dr Amy Ludlow. It brings university students into prisons across the UK to learn alongside incarcerated people.

9   'London Bridge Terrorist Preached with ISIS Flag After Being Bullied at School,' Chris Caulfield, *Metro*, 30 November 2019, https://metro.co.uk/2019/11/30/london-bridge-terrorist-preached-with-isis-flag-after-being-bullied-at-school-11247590/.

10   HMP Whitemoor is a high security prison for Category A and B adult male prisoners serving different kinds of sentences, of over four years. Category A is the highest risk an individual can be known as. See *An exploration of staff-prisoner relationships at HMP Whitemoor: 12 years on*, Alison Leibling, Helen Arnold and Christina Straub, Cambridge Institute of Criminology, Prisons Research Centre, November 2011.

11   'London Bridge Terror Picture Emerges of Attacker with Islamist Hate Preacher,' Anjem Choudhary, Sky News, 3 December 2019, https://news.sky.com/story/london-bridge-terror-picture-emerges-of-attacker-with-isla-mist-hate-preacher-anjem-choudary-11876967.

12   Leibling et al, *Ibid*.

13   'Fact Sheet: Desistance and Disengagement Programme,' UK Home Office, 5 November 2019, https://homeofficemedia.blog.gov.uk/2019/11/05/fact-sheet-desistance-and-disengagement-programme/ .

14   'The Ultra-Ultra Violence,' Erwin James, *Guardian,* 27 February 2009, https://www.theguardian.com/film/2009/feb/27/charles-bronson-vio-lence-criminal-justice.

15   Maya Angelou, in the context of not judging people on preconceived ideas.

16   FHI Day 2, 13 April 2021, https://fishmongershallinquests.independent.gov.uk/wp-content/uploads/2021/04/FHI-Day-2-13-April-2021.pdf.

17   'London Bridge Attack: Usman Khan's Lawyer Admits He Could Have Been Deceived,' Jonathan Ames, *The Sunday Times*, 2 December 2019.

18   'The Guardian and Erwin James,, Ian Katz, *Guardian*, April 2009. Katz writes about the decision to give 'James' (real name Erwin James Monahan) the platform under a pseudonym, and how it was received, and what the impact was on James. 'He seemed to be a walking, talking testimony to the power of redemption… But beyond his writing, James's own life began to take on the quality of a modern parable. In the years since his release in 2004, James has continued his remarkable journey of rehabilitation.

'At times, it has had an almost too-good-to-be-true quality about it, and perhaps no one should have been surprised that this extraordinary journey should take the odd disappointing turn. The fictionalised paragraphs in his pieces about his time in the Foreign Legion - as detailed in today's corrections column - were, I am convinced, an isolated lapse by someone who has otherwise dedicated himself to, as he puts it, "being authentic". *What is clear to me is that this blot on his post-conviction copybook was somehow born of his struggle to keep his two lives apart*' (italics mine), https://www.theguardian.com/theguardian/2009/apr/24/erwin-james-monahan-guardian.

19   The second in four years. UK general elections are usually held every five years.

20   John Crilly, Darryn Frost, Steven Gallant, Marc Conway and Lukasz Koczocik have become known worldwide for their actions that day. Polish Lukasz, who was first aid trained and was working as a kitchen porter in Fishmongers' Hall, Marc ex-prisoner convicted of serious crime now employed at the UK charity, The Prison Reform Trust, John, managing heroin addiction and once wrongly convicted under the UK's pernicious 'joint enterprise' law for murder – had spent 13 years in prison where he met Jack, and completed a Law degree via Learning Together. He is one of the rare people in the UK ever to have a JE conviction overturned, and is now a passionate campaigner for people in similar circumstances through the organisation JENGbA – Joint Enterprise, Not Guilty by Association, https://jointenterprise.co/. Darryn – a civil servant in HM Prison and Probation Service, only at the event as a last minute fill-in for a colleague who could not make it – now campaigning through an organisation he set up, 'Extinguish Hate' https://www.extinguishhate.co.uk/. Stephen Gallant was incarcerated for murder, but was on day release for the LT event; he eventually had his sentence reduced by order of the Queen, though his victim's family suffered recurrent PTSD as this was in process. https://www.thetimes.co.uk/article/steve-gallant-queen-steps-in-to-help-release-london-bridge-attack-hero-10-months-early-75mrq79r9 Steve, Marc, and John had participated in LT courses and knew Jack. Crilly recalls: 'We was heroes at first, eh – then it found we was prisoners and it just went pmp.' *Prison Break, Episode 5: If Not This, Then What?* BBC Radio 4, 21 May 2021.

21   Statement of the family of Saskia Jones to the inquest, 12 April 2021, p.23. The statement in full reads, 'It is very important to the family that Saskia's legacy should not solely be based on her work with Learning Together, as she was about so much more than just that. She should be defined as someone who battled to improve the lives of others in several spheres and was driven to make real changes in the world. Her incredible research in the field of sexual violence with Rape Crisis Cambridge more than shapes part of that legacy. Her passion in this area enabled her to finally find her career path, with the hope of becoming a detective in victim support with the police force.' FHI-PR, April 12 2021 https://fishmongershallinquests.independent.gov.uk/wp-content/uploads/2021/04/FHI-Day-1-12-April-2021.pdf.

22   FHI-PR, 16 October 2020.

23   It is not the purpose or place of this book to speculate on what motivated Khan to commit this attack, or his relationship to, or his ideological position (or his personal thoughts) on suicide and how those connected to his decisions that day.

24   *Diving into the Wreck: Poems 1971-1972*, Adrienne Rich (USA: Norton, 1973), p.372.

25   *Diving into the Wreck*, Rich, p.372.

26   Diversity Form (UK) Q.E: *What is your ethnic origin?*

27   *Axiomatic*, Maria Tumarkin (USA: Transit Books, 2019), p.93.

28   *What Is Found There,* Adrienne Rich (USA: WW Norton, 2003), p.181.

29   *What is Found There*, Rich, p.181.

30   'Cartographies of Silence,' in *Collected Poems: 1950-2012*, Adrienne Rich (USA: Norton, 2016).

31   *Collected Poems*, Rich, p.107.

32   *Collected Poems*, Rich, p.183.

33   'If I Told Him, A Completed Portrait of Picasso,' Gertrude Stein, *Poetry Foundation*, https://www.poetryfoundation.org/poems/55215/if-i-told-him-a-completed-portrait-of-picasso.

34   *Axiomatic*, Tumarkin, p. 48-49.

35   'Avert the Icy Feeling,' in *Threads*, Bhanu Kapil (UK: Clinic Publishing, 2008), p.54.

36   *Axiomatic*, Tumarkin, p.48-49.

37   FHI-PIR-16, October 2020, https://fishmongershallinquests.independent. gov.uk/documents/.

38   *The Muslims are Coming!*, Arun Kundnani (UK: Verso, 2015), p.289.

39   *The Muslims are Coming!*, Kundnani.

40   *Pedagogy of the Oppressed*, Paulo Freire (UK: Penguin Classics, 2017).

41   *The Muslims are Coming!*, Kundnani.

42   *The 'Desegregation' of English Schools*, Oliver Esteves (UK: Manchester University Press, 2018), p.16.

43   'Introduction,' Lauren Elkin, in *Translation as Transhumance*, Mireille Gansel, trans. Ros Schwartz (UK: Les Fugitives, 2017), p.viii.

44   *The 'Desegregation' of English Schools,* Esteves, p.109 original quote from an article by Coard in *Guardian*, 4 May 1971.

45   *The 'Desegregation' of English Schools,* Esteves, p.15.

46   'How Black Working Class Youth Are Criminalized and Excluded in the English School System,' Jessica Perera, Institute of Race Relations, 28 September 2020, https://irr.org.uk/article/beyond-the-pru-to-prison-pipeline/.

       See also, 'Discrimination at school: is a Black British history lesson repeating itself?' Lola Okolosie, *Guardian,* 15 November 2020, https://www.theguardian.com/education/2020/nov/15/discrimination-at-school-is-a-black-british-history-lesson-repeating-itself-small-axe-education-steve-mcqueen

47   'More Black People Jailed in England and Wales Proportionally than in US,' Randeep Ramesh, Guardian, 10 October 2020, https://www.theguardian. com/society/2010/oct/11/black-prison-population-increase-england.

48   'Joint Enterprise Criminalises Young BAME People,' Russell Webster, 5 February 2016, https://www.russellwebster.com/joint-enterprise-racism/

49   'Racial Bias Is Pulling Young Black Adults into the Revolving Door,' Russell Webster, 10 August 2020, https://www.russellwebster.com/racial-bias-revolving-door/

50   'Racial Bias Is Pulling Young Black Adults into the Revolving Door,' Russell Webster, 10 August 2020, https://www.russellwebster.com/racial-bias-revolving-door/.

51   'An Independent Review Into the Treatment Of, and Outcomes For Black, Asian and Minority Ethnic individuals in the Criminal Justice System,' David Lammy, *The Lammy Review*, (UK: Ministry of Justice, 2017), p.3. https://assets.publishing.service.gov.uk/government/uploads/system/uploads/attachment_data/file/643001/lammy-review-final-report.pdf.

52   *Diving into the Wreck*, Rich.

53   *Cold Dark Matter: An Exploded View*, Cornelia Parker (1991), https://www.tate.org.uk/art/artworks/parker-cold-dark-matter-an-exploded-view-t06949/story-cold-dark-matter.

54   About the poem 'Popular Culture, Cruel Work,' Wendy Trevino, Poets.org, https://poets.org/poem/popular-culture-cruel-work.

55   Transcript, *Inquests Into the Deaths Arising From the Fishmongers' Hall and London Bridge Terror Attack*, Day 1, 25 March, 2021, https://www.opus2.com.

56   The play was about a terrorist committing a knife attack. It was not written during my course and I had no knowledge of it until the inquest made it public in the inquest process. The inquests also revealed that MI5 had a copy of the play, and considered it simply creative writing as a marker of rehabilitation.

57   *Dark Days,* James Baldwin (UK: Penguin Modernisms, 2018), p.19.

58   *Living a Feminist Life*, Ahmed, p.261.

59   *Azadi: Freedom. Fascism. Fiction.*, Arundhati Roy (UK: Penguin Random House, 2020), p.108.

60   'A Pattern Marks London Terror Attacks,' Luv Puri, *The Tribune,* 4 December 2019, https://www.tribuneindia.com/news/archive/comment/a-pattern-marks-london-terror-attacks-869772.

61   See, for example, 'The Myth of Return,' *Lancashire Telegraph*, 24 January 2006, https://www.lancashiretelegraph.co.uk/news/6236312.myth-return/.

62   'The Pakistani Muslim Community in England,' Department for Communities and Local Government, March 2009, https://webarchive.nationalarchives.gov.uk/20120920001118/ and http://www.communities.gov.uk/documents/communities/pdf/1170952.pdf.

63   'Rivers of Blood,' a speech made by Conservative MP Enoch Powell in 1968, attacking the UK's open immigration policy. Often understood as a pioneering work of ethno-nationalism, it was inspired by its author's experience in colonial India, when the long practice of divide and rule fuelled communal violence at Partition. See 'India, Post Imperialism and the origins of Enoch Powell's *Rivers of Blood* Speech', Paul Foster, *The Historical Journal 50*(3), p. 669-687, https://www.cambridge.org/core/journals/historical-journal/article/abs/india-postimperialism-and-the-origins-of-enoch-powells-rivers-of-blood-speech/3BFC82A807D920B152BE-F300BEB21FC3.

64   'In Memory of WB Yeats,' WH Auden, https://poets.org/poem/memory-w-b-yeats.

65   Title poem, *The Country Without A Post Office*, Agha Shahid Ali, originally published as 'Kashmir without a Post Office' (USA: Norton, 1998).

66   'In Memory of WB Yeats,' Auden.

67   *Climate of Fear*, Wole Soyinka (UK: Profile Books, 2014), p.74.

68   *Until We Reckon: Violence, Mass Incarceration and the Road to Repair*, Danielle Sered (USA: The New Press, 2019), p.11.

69   *Climate of Fear*, Soyinka, p.75.

70   *Climate of Fear*, Soyinka.

71   12-year-old refugee Shukri Abdi died by drowning when she was with a group of peers. She could not swim, and had been extensively bullied at school. https://www.theguardian.com/uk-news/2020/jun/10/shukri-abdi-burnham-calls-for-wider-investigation-over-drowning-of-12-year-old-refugee.

72   'Education in Jails Undermined by London Bridge Attack,' Sarah Marsh, *Guardian*, 1 December 2019, https://www.theguardian.com/uk-news/2019/dec/01/education-jails-not-undermined-london-bridge-attack [accessed 23 December 2020].

73   FHI-PR.

74   'We the Heartbroken,' Gargi Bhattacharya, https://www.plutobooks.com/blog/we-the-heartbroken/.

75   'On the Language of Nonviolence and the US Criminal Justice System,' Michael Fischer, *Literary Hub*, 2 November 2020, https://lithub.com/on-the-language-of-nonviolence-and-the-us-criminal-justice-system/.

76   *The Muslims are Coming!*, Kundnani, p.289.

77   '7 July London Bombings: The World on a Train, 10 Years On,' Geoff Ryman, BBC, 6 July 2015, https://www.bbc.co.uk/news/magazine-33384595.

78   Tawseef Khan, interview with Krishnan Guru Murthy, *Ways to Change the World With Krishnan Guru Murthy*, https://waystochangetheworld.libsyn.com/tawseef-khan-on-islamophobia-integration-and-what-he-calls-the-muslim-problem.

79   See, for example, *Cut from the Same Cloth*, ed. Sabeena Akhtar (UK, Unbound: 2021), *I Refuse to Condemn: Resisting Racism in a Time of National Security*, ed. Asim Qureshi (Manchester University Press, 2020), *The Muslims Are Coming!*, Arun Kundnani (London: Verso, 2014), or *We Need New Stories*, Nesrine Malik (UK: W&N, 2020).

80   *The Waves*, Virginia Woolf (UK: Penguin Modern Classics, 2003), p.3.

81   London Borough of Newham, Demographics 2020, https://en.wikipedia.org/wiki/London_Borough_of_Newham#Religion.

82   'Capitalism Has Become a Weapon of Mass Destruction: Seven Questions with Arundhati Roy,' Emily Tamkin, *The New Statesman*, 8 April 2021, https://www.newstatesman.com/world/asia/2021/04/capitalism-has-become-weapon-mass-destruction-seven-questions-arundhati-roy.

83   'UK Remains the World's Second Biggest Arms Exporter with 11bn of Orders,' Dan Sabbagh, *Guardian*, 6 October 2020, https://www.theguardian.com/world/2020/oct/06/uk-remains-second-biggest-arms-exporter-with-11bn-of-orders.

84   'It's Time for America to Reckon with the Staggering Death Toll of the Post 9/11 Wars,' Murtaza Hussain, 19 November 2018, https://theintercept. com/2018/11/19/civilian-casualties-us-war-on-terror/.

85   'A Litany for Survival No. 42,' in *The Collected Poems of Audre Lorde*, Audre Lorde (W.W. Norton, 1997).

86   See *Assimilation, Exodus, Eradication, Iraq's Minorities Since 2003*, Preti Taneja (London: MRG, 2006), *Uncertain Refuge, Dangerous Return: Iraq's Uprooted Minorities*, Chris Chapman and Preti Taneja (London: MRG, 2009), *Iraq's Minorities: Participation in Public Life*, Preti Taneja (London: MRG, 2011).

87   Selections from *Citizen: An American Lyric*, Claudia Rankine, pp. 15 and 131-133. Copyright © 2014 by Claudia Rankine. Used with the permission of The Permissions Company,LLC on behalf of Graywolf Press, graywolf-press.org.

88   *Citizen*, Rankine.

89   Excerpt from 'Faceless' from *Heaven is All Goodbyes,* Tongo Eisen-Martin. Copyright © 2017 by Tongo Eisen-Martin. Reprinted with the permission of The Permissions Company, LLC on behalf of City Lights Books, citylights.com.

90   From the poem by Rabindranath Tagore, trans. Gayatri Spivak, 'Ethics and Politics in Tagore, Coetzee and Certain Scenes of Teaching,' *Diacritics* 32 (3/4):17-31 (2002).

91   FHI-PR.

92   'When We Come to It,' Maya Angelou, https://www.youtube.com/ watch?v=UjEfq7wLm7M.

93   *Some of Us Did Not Die: New and Selected Essays,* June Jordan (USA: Basic/ Civitas Books, 2002) p.265 (italics hers).

94   *Trust and Violence*, Jan Philipp Reemtsma, trans. Dominic Bonfiglio (USA: Princeton University Press, 2012) p.1-4.

95   *Trust and Violence*, Reemstma, p.7.

96   *Precarious Life: The Powers of Mourning and Violence*, Judith Butler (London: Verso, 2004), p.10.

97   See Glossary: *Funny Tinge*.

98   'Terrorism,' *OurWorldInData.org*, Hannah Ritchie, Joe Hasell, Cameron
        Appel and Max Roser (2013), https://ourworldindata.org/terrorism.

99   'Grappling with Shadows,' Lowkey in *I Refuse to Condemn*, ed. Asim
        Qureshi, (UK: Manchester University Press, 2021), p.203-204.

100   'Miner's Strike Was Bitter and Hard Fought,' Richard Ault, *Stoke Sentinel*, 28
        August 2017, https://www.stokesentinel.co.uk/news/history/miners-strike-
        bitter-hard-fought-389935.

101   For an interesting and important discussion of this term in the context of
        9/11, see: 'Islam's New Native Informant,' Nesrine Malik, *New York Review
        of Books*, 7 June 2018, https://www.nybooks.com/daily/2018/06/07/is-
        lams-new-native-informants/.

102   Labour MP Florence Eshalomi asks Priti Patel about structural racism in the
        UK, Channel 4 News, 8 June 2020, https://www.facebook.com/Channel-
        4News/videos/labour-mp-florence-eshalomi-asks-priti-patel-about-structu-
        ral-racism-in-the-uk/250342173079880/.

103   *We Do This 'Til We Free Us*, Mariame Kaba (USA: Haymarket Books,
        2021), p.24.

104   'Prison Population Set to Hit 10000,' *Inside Time*, 30th November, 2020,
        https://insidetime.org/prison-population-set-to-hit-100000/.

105   'Angela Smith Has Left Labour. Who Do I Complain to About Her "Fun-
        ny Tinge" Comment?' Ash Sarkar, *Guardian*, 19 February 2019, https://
        www.theguardian.com/commentisfree/2019/feb/19/angela-smith-left-la-
        bour-funny-tinge-mp-racism.

106   'Rethinking Our Criminal Justice System: Understanding Abolition in the
        UK,' Hajera Begum, *Amaliah*, 15 March 2020, https://www.amaliah.com/
        post/59631/rethinking-justice-system-understanding-abolition-uk.

107   'Intervening Effectively with Terrorist Offenders,' Chris Dean, *Prison Service
        Journal,* Issue 203, p.31-36.

108   Bob Lambert, Undercover Police Officer, Wikipedia, https://en.wikipedia.org/
        wiki/Bob_Lambert_(undercover_police_officer).

109   See especially *Until We Reckon*, Danielle Sered (USA: The New Press, 2019).

110   *Inquests Into the Deaths Arising From the Fishmongers' Hall and London Bridge Terror Attack*, Opus 2, Official Court Reporters, (March 25, 2021,) p.5.

111   'Hope is a Discipline,' Mariame Kaba with Brian Sonenstein and Kim Wilson, *Beyond Prisons* Ep.19, https://www.stitcher.com/podcast/beyond-prisons/e/53864185.

112   For the full description of Khan's sentencing and release with restrictions trajectory, see 'Usman Khan and sentencing terror offences,' *Full Fact*, 11 December 2019 https://fullfact.org/election-2019/terror-attack-sentencing-usman-khan/.

113   'Fastest Growing Terrorist Threat Is From the Far Right, Say Police,' Vikram Dodd and Jamie Grierson, 19 September, 2019 https://www.theguardian.com/uk-news/2019/sep/19/fastest-growing-uk-terrorist-threat-is-from-far-right-say-police.

114   'Harry Vaughan: House of Lords Clerk's Son a neo-Nazi Satanist,' Daniel De Simone, BBC News, 16 October 2020, https://www.bbc.co.uk/news/uk-england-london-54568916.

115   'Don't Expand the War on Terror in the Name of Antiracism,' Arun Kundnani and Jeane Theoharis, *Jacobin,* 1 November 2019, https://www.jacobinmag.com/2019/11/war-on-terror-domestic-terrorism-act-racism-muslims.

116   'Terror and Abolition,' Atiya Husain, *Boston Review*, 11 June, 2020, http://bostonreview.net/race/atiya-husain-terror-and-abolition.

117   'If Not This, Then What?' Dr David Scott, *Prison Break*, *Ep.5*, BBC Sounds, 21 May 2021, https://www.bbc.co.uk/sounds/play/m000w5vh.

118   'Counter Terror Chief Says Policing Alone Cannot Beat Extremism,' Vikram Dodd, *Guardian*, 16 August 2019, https://www.theguardian.com/uk-news/2019/aug/06/counter-terrorism-chief-calls-for-greater-social-inclusion.

119   'Tougher Sentencing and Monitoring Overall in Government Overhaul of Terrorism Response,' UK Home Office news story, 21 January 2021, https://www.gov.uk/government/news/tougher-sentencing-and-monitoring-in-government-overhaul-of-terrorism-response.

120   *We Do This 'Til We Free Us*, Kaba, p.25.

121   'A Reader's War,' in *Known and Strange Things,* Teju Cole (UK: Faber and Faber, 2016), p.258-259.

122   'What is To Be Done?' Ruth Wilson Gilmore, *American Quarterly*, June 2011, Vol. 63, No. 2, June 2011 p.245-265, p.258.

123   'Yih faṣl umīdon kī hamdam,' *Zindān Nāmah* (*Prison Narrative*), Faiz Ahmed Faiz (Dehli: Kabīr Buk Ḍipo, 1955), p. 132-34.

124   'Responding to What is Literary Activism,' Wendy Trevino, Juliana Spahr, Tim Kreiner, Joshua Clover. Chris Chen, Jasper Bernes, Poetry Foundation, https://www.poetryfoundation.org/harriet-books/2015/08/responding-to-what-is-literary-activism.

125   *Known and Strange Things*, Cole, p.78-92.

126   *Not to Read*, Alejandro Zambra, trans. Megan McDowell (UK: Fitzcarraldo Editions, 2018), p.249.

127   'Caliban Blues,' Daniel Swift, *Public Books*, 5 July 2017, https://www.publicbooks.org/caliban-blues/.

128   'Caliban Blues,' Swift. 'Atwood reinstates precisely the troubling political hierarchies that the play exposed and postcolonial critics and directors have found so productive.'

129   'Minute on Indian Education,' 1835, Thomas Babington Macaulay.

130   'Caliban Blues,' Swift.

131   *The Tempest*, William Shakespeare (I.ii.366–368).

132   *Hip Hop & Shakespeare?* Akala, TedxAldeburgh, 7 December 2011, https://www.youtube.com/watch?v=DSbtkLA3GrY.

133   'We Lived in the Blank White Spaces: Rewriting the Paradigm of Denial in Atwood's *The Handmaid's Tale*,' Danita J. Dodson, *Utopian Studies*, 1997, Vol. 8, No. 2 (1997) (USA: Penn State University Press), p.66-86, https://www.jstor.org/stable/20719685.

134   *Corrections and Conditional Release 2019*, Public Safety Canada, https://www.
        publicsafety.gc.ca/cnt/rsrcs/pblctns/ccrso-2019/ccrso-2019-en.pdf [accessed
        3 April 2021] p.69.

135   'Black Canadians and the Justice System,' Anthony N. Morgan, *Policy
        Options*, 8 May 2018, https://policyoptions.irpp.org/magazines/may-2018/
        black-canadians-justice-system/.

136   See, for example, 'Who Liberates the Slaves?' Sophie Lewis, *The White
        Review*, December 2019, https://www.thewhitereview.org/reviews/who-
        liberates-the-slaves/.

137   'Get Out of Gilead: Anti-Blackness in *The Handmaid's Tale*,' Priya Nair,
        Bitch Media, 14 April 2017, https://www.bitchmedia.org/article/anti-black-
        ness-handmaids-tale.

138   'Caliban Blues,' Swift.

139   *Teaching to Transgress, Education as the Practice of Freedom*, bell hooks (UK:
        Routledge, 1994), p.91.

140   'Author and Hero in Aesthetic Activity,' Mikhail Bakhtin, in *Art and Answer-
        ability: Early Philosophical Essays*, trans. Vadim Liapunov (USA: University of
        Texas Press, 1990), p.16.

141   'Intensity of a Plot,' Marc Binelli, *Guernica*, https://www.guernicamag.com/
        intensity_of_a_plot/.

142   'Laureate of Terror,' Martin Amis, *The New Yorker*, 21 November 2011,
        https://www.newyorker.com/magazine/2011/11/21/laureate-of-terror.

143   *Tragedy Since 9/11, Reading a World Out of Joint*, Jennifer Wallace (UK: Cam-
        bridge University Press, 2019), p.41.

144   *Mao II*, Don DeLillo (New York: Penguin, 1991). Used by permission of
        Don DeLillo and the Robin Straus Agency, Inc.

145   'The Ascendance of Don DeLillo,' Jonathan Bing, *Publisher's Week-
        ly*, 11 August 1997, https://www.publishersweekly.com/pw/
        print/19970811/22663-the-ascendance-of-don-delillo.html.

146   *Life Imprisonment from Young Adulthood: Adaptation, Identity and Time*, Ben
        Crewe, Susie Huley and Serena Wright (UK: Palgrave, 2020), p. 328.

147   See, for example, *Totality and Infinity: An Essay on Exteriority*, Emmanuel
        Levinas, tr. Alphonso Lingis, (Dordrecht: KluwerAcademic Publishers,
        1991).

148   *Precarious Life: The Powers of Mourning and Violence*, Judith Butler (London:
        Verso, 2004), p.10.

149   *The Reluctant Fundamentalist*, Mohsin Hamid (UK: Hamish Hamilton, 2007),
        back cover blurb, Rachel Cooke, *New Statesman*.

150   The director Mira Nair's emphatic changing of the story and ending to
        confirming the narrator is 'a good guy' in her 2014 film adaptation shows
        how times change; and confirms the author's original intentions that readers
        believe the narrator – if not holding the knife – is at least directly involved.

151   *Weddings and Beheadings*, Hanif Kureishi, *Prospect,* 19 November 2006,
        https://www.prospectmagazine.co.uk/magazine/weddingsbeheadings

152   'Assimilation, Exodus, Eradication: Iraq's Minority Communities Since
        2003,' Preti Taneja, Minority Rights Group International (2007), https://
        minorityrights.org/publications/assimilation-exodus-eradication-iraqs-mi-
        nority-communities-since-2003-february-2007/.

153   See *Life Imprisonment*, Crewe et al.

154   *Teaching to Transgress*, hooks, p.167.

155   Ben Jarman, University of Cambridge. Note supplied to the author.

156   'Leaks Leave Priti Patel's Asylum Plans All at Sea,' George Parker and
        Robert Wright, *Financial Times*, 1 October 2020, https://www.ft.com/con-
        tent/989c200f-8bc8-4482-9ce8-18375468f104

157   With thanks to Ben Jarman for help with shaping this section. Any mistakes
        are mine.

158   'Government Considers Single Supermax Jail to House Islamic Terrorists,'
        Alan Travis, *Guardian*, 14 February 2016, https://www.theguardian.com/soci-
        ety/2016/feb/12/government-considers-single-supermax-jail-islamist-terrorists

159   'Inside Britain's Close Supervision Units, Prisons Within Prisons,' *Corporate
        Watch*, https://corporatewatch.org/inside-britains-close-supervision-cen-
        tres-prisons-within-prisons/.

160   'Community Action on Prison Expansion,' Cape Campaign, https://
        cape-campaign.org/nationaldemo/.

161   *Cherry*, Nico Walker (USA: Knopf, 2018), p.9.

162   'Hopefully He Won't End Up Robbing Banks Again: The Wild Life of
        Nico Walker,' Nate Rogers, *The Ringer*, 11 March 2021, https://www.
        theringer.com/2021/3/11/22321723/nico-walker-cherry-movie-au-
        thor-russo-brothers-adaptation.

163   *The Ringer*, Rogers.

164   'The Hooker Laureate of the Dirtbag Left,' Kaitlin Philips, *The Cut*, 12
        November 2019, https://www.thecut.com/2019/11/rachel-rabbit-white-
        poetry-book-launch-party.html.

165   'They Swore to Protect America. Some Also Joined the Riot,' Rob Kuznia
        and Ashley Fantz, *CNN Investigates*, 15 January 2021, https://edition.cnn.
        com/2021/01/12/us/military-extremism-capitol-riot-invs/index.html.

166   Italicised text from the back cover copy of *Outline*, Rachel Cusk (USA:
        Picador, 2014).

167   'Why Is Anti-protest Bill Generating So Much Controversy?' Haroon
        Siddiqi and Matthew Weaver, *Guardian*, 22 March 2021, https://www.
        theguardian.com/uk-news/2021/mar/15/why-is-anti-protest-bill-generat-
        ing-so-much-controversy.

168   'Before This I Had Never Won a Raffle' Tayari Jones, *Guardian*, 9 June,
        2019, https://www.theguardian.com/books/2019/jun/09/womens-prize-
        winner-tayari-jones-before-this-i-had-never-won-a-raffle.

169   *Guardian*, Jones.

170   *An American Marriage*, Tayari Jones (UK: Oneworld, 2018), p.300.

171   Title and form from three sources.
        1. *Reality Hunger,* David Shields, (USA: Knopf, 2010), whose cover asks, 'Is
        art theft?' The book 'contains hundreds of quotations that go unacknowledged
        in the body of the text… However Random House lawyers determined that
        it was necessary for me to provide a complete list of citations; the list follows
        (except for any sources I couldn't find or forgot along the way.' p.209.

2. Joint enterprise is 'a doctrine of criminal law which permits two or more defendants to be convicted of the same criminal offence in relation to the same incident, even where they had different types or levels of involvement in the incident.' See https://jointenterprise.co/

3. The full articulation of 'a killjoy manifesto' can be found in *Living a Feminist Life*, Sara Ahmed (London: Duke University Press, 2017), p.252.

The citations for this section are therefore included with personal reflection where appropriate.

172 *Living a Feminist Life*, Ahmed.

173 'Black Women in the UK Four Times More Likely to Die in Pregnancy or Childbirth,' Hannah Summers, *Guardian*, 15 January 2021, https://www. theguardian.com/global-development/2021/jan/15/black-women-in-the-uk-four-times-more-likely-to-die-in-pregnancy-or-childbirth. Why start here? Because we have to begin somewhere.

174 *Guardian*, Summers.

175 *Guardian*, Summers.

176 'Coronoavirus: Higher Ethnic Death Not Linked to Health,' https://www. bbc.co.uk/news/health-54567866.

177 *Joint Enterprise: Righting a Wrong Turn?*, Jessica Jacobson, Amy Kirby, Gillian Hunter, Institute of Criminal Policy Research, University of London, (UK: London, Prison Reform Trust, 2016), http://www.prisonreformtrust. org.uk/Portals/0/Documents/Joint%20Enterprise%20Writing%20a%20 Wrong%20Turn.pdf.

178 'Lonely Man in Space,' Learning Together writer, *Visual Verse* Vol 6, Ch 5. https://visualverse.org/submissions/lonely-man-in-space/ [accessed 8, Feb 2021] *Visual Verse* is an online anthology of art and words co founded by Kristen Harrison, The Curved House, and the author in 2013. It invites lead writers and then writers worldwide to respond to an image with a piece of writing of 50-500 words, completed in the space of an hour. The Writing Together class of 2018 took part in the challenge. Following the prison protocol on publication, the work of all the writers was published anonymously. Excerpts were selected randomly for this piece.

179   *Living a Feminist Life*, Ahmed, p.252.

180   'The Spaceman,' Learning Together writer, *Visual Verse*, Vol 6, Ch.5, https://visualverse.org/submissions/the-spaceman/.

181   'Exploring Ethnic Inequalities in Admissions to Russel Group Universities,' Vicky Boliver, *Sociology*, 2016, https://journals.sagepub.com/doi/full/10.1177/0038038515575859.

182   'Man in Space,' Learning Together writer, *Visual Verse*, Vol 6. Ch.5, https://visualverse.org/submissions/man-in-space/.

183   *Living a Feminist Life*, Ahmed, p.252.

184   'I Need My Own Space in Space,' Learning Together writer, *Visual Verse*, Vol.6 Ch.5, https://visualverse.org/submissions/i-need-my-own-space-in-space/.

185   'The Joint Enterprise Law Has Changed. But Still We Must Fight to Free Our Sons,' Sally Halsall, *Guardian*, 7 September 2016, https://www.theguardian.com/commentisfree/2016/sep/07/joint-enterpirse-law-changed-fighting-black-minority-crime.

186   *Guardian*, Okolosie.

187   *Prison Narrative*, Faiz Ahmed Faiz, p.117.

188   *Living a Feminist Life*, Ahmed, p.252.

189   The 'Evaluating the Personal, Interpersonal and Contextual' (EPIC) scale, is a tool for assessing the impact of Learning Together's participatory model of education between prisons and universities, on the students who took part. The scale was formulated by the co-founders of LT, Dr Ruth Armstrong and Dr Amy Ludlow. https://www.prisonerseducation.org.uk/2021/03/evaluating-the-personal-interpersonal-and-contextual-dimensions-of-growth-through-learning-together/.

190   'Prisoners' Childhood Family Backgrounds,' Kim Williams, Vea Papadopoulou and Natalie Booth, *Ministry of Justice Research Series*, March 2012. https://assets.publishing.service.gov.uk/government/uploads/system/uploads/attachment_data/file/278837/prisoners-childhood-family-backgrounds.pdf.

191 *Antigone*, Sophocles (4.4.42-44).

192 *Lammy Review*, Lammy.

193 'I'm Not There,' Learning Together writer, *Visual Verse*, Vol. 6 Ch.5, https://visualverse.org/submissions/im-not-there/.

194 'Destiny,' Learning Together writer, *Visual Verse* Vol.6 Ch.5, https://visualverse.org/submissions/destiny-learning-together/.

195 'Joint Enterprise,' Webster.

196 'Look Like You,' Grizzy x M Dargg, https://www.youtube.com/watch?v=pHfKPoSgSSc.

197 Disclaimer, HBVTV, screen 'Look Like You,' Grizzy x M Dargg, https://www.youtube.com/watch?v=pHfKPoSgSSc.

198 David Shields, interview with Sean Carman, *The Rumpus,* 7 March 2013, https://therumpus.net/2013/03/the-rumpus-interview-with-david-shields-2/.

199 *Comedy of Errors*, William Shakespeare, IV. 3, a play rife with doubles, exile and the solitary.

200 'Prisoners' Childhood Family Backgrounds,' Williams et al.

201 It's a question of numbers, demographics, and so on.

202 *An American Marriage*, Jones.

203 *An American Marriage*, Jones, p.4.

204 'Destiny,' Learning Together writer.

205 *Living a Feminist Life*, Ahmed, p.252.

206 'I'm not there,' Learning Together Writer, *Visual Verse*, Vol 6. Ch. 5, https://visualverse.org/submissions/im-not-there/.

207 'Prisoners' Childhood Family Backgrounds,' Williams et al.

208 'Floating,' Learning Together writer, *Visual Verse*, Vol.6 Ch.5, https://visualverse.org/submissions/floating-learning-together/.

209 *Empire's Endgame, Racism and the British State,* Gargi Bhattacharya, Adam Elliotts-Cooper, Sita Balani, Kerem Nişancıoğlu, Kojo Koram, Dalia Gebrial,

Nadine El El-Enany, Luke De Noronha (UK: Pluto Press 2021), p.9.

210   *This Little Art*, Kate Briggs (UK: Fitzcarraldo Editions, 2017), p.271.

211   A Cambridge website describing Learning Together. It has been archived since the attack.

212   *all about love*, bell hooks (USA: Harper Collins, 2001), p.91.

213   *Água Viva*, Clarice Lispector, trans. Stefan Tobler (USA: New Directions, 2012), p.72

214   'Jailed Turkish Author Ahmet Altan Freed After Three Years,' Alison Flood, *Guardian*, 6 November 2019, https://www.theguardian.com/books/2019/nov/06/jailed-turkish-author-ahmet-altan-freed-after-three-years.

215   See, for example, 'United Kingdom: UN Condems "Reprehensible" Racism Report,' OHCHR, 19 April 2021, https://www.ohchr.org/EN/NewsEvents/Pages/DisplayNews.aspx?NewsID=27005&LangID=E [accessed 21 April, 2021], and 'Race Report: UK Not Deliberately Rigged Against Ethnic Minorities,' BBC News, 1 April 2021, https://www.bbc.co.uk/news/uk-56585538.

216   *We Do This 'Til We Free Us*, Kaba, p.197.

PRETI TANEJA is a writer and activist. Her first novel, *We That Are Young* (Galley Beggar Press/Knopf), won the Desmond Elliott Prize for the UK's best debut of the year and was listed for international awards, including the Folio Prize, the Prix Jan Michalski, and the Shakti Bhatt First Book Prize. It has been translated into several languages. Taneja lectures in creative writing at Newcastle University and broadcasts on world literature and culture for the BBC.

Undelivered Lectures is a narrative nonfiction series featuring book-length essays in slim, handsome editions.

Transit Books is a nonprofit publisher of international and American literature, based in Oakland, California. Founded in 2015, Transit Books is committed to the discovery and promotion of enduring works that carry readers across borders and communities. Visit us online to learn more about our forthcoming titles, events, and opportunities to support our mission.

TRANSITBOOKS.ORG